Informed Dissent:
Three Generals & the Viet Nam War

VIETNAM GENERATION, INC.
&
Burning Cities Press

VIETNAM GENERATION

Vietnam Generation, Inc. was founded in 1988 to promote and encourage interdisciplinary study of the Vietnam War era and the Vietnam War generation. The journal is published by Vietnam Generation, Inc., a nonprofit corporation devoted to promoting scholarship on recent history and contemporary issues.

Vietnam Generation, Inc.

All correspondence, including manuscript submissions, should be sent to Kali Tal, Editor, *Vietnam Generation*, 2921 Terrace Dr., Chevy Chase, MD 20815; (301) 608-0622; FAX: (301) 608-0761. Style sheets may be requested from the editor. If you wish your submission returned, please enclose SASE. Subscriptions to *Vietnam Generation* are $40. per year for individuals, and $75 per year for institutions. (Add $12 postage for subscriptions outside the US.) Single copies may be purchased at $12. per issue, or at $9 per issue for orders of over 10. All orders must be prepaid in US currency. Please notify us of change of address at least six weeks in advance; there is a charge for replacement of issues which are returned by the Post Office as undeliverable at the address shown. If claims for undelivered issues are made within six months of the publication date, we will replace the journal. We do not accept cancellations or provide refunds. *Vietnam Generation* is published quarterly, in January, April, July, and October. Copies of the *Vietnam Generation Newsletter* and access to the Vietnam Generation bibliographic database are included in the purchase price of the subscription.

ISSN: 1042-7597
ISBN: 0-9628524-4-9

Contents

Informed Dissent: Three Generals and the Viet Nam War

Dan Duffy

Here are two essays about generals.

Robert Buzzanco writes principally of James Gavin (Army) and David Shoup (Marine Corps), military leaders who opposed the growing U.S. commitment to the Republic of Viet Nam while in the service in the early 1960s. After retiring from their military careers and entering public life later in the decade, they became two of the most vocal critics of the U.S. war effort. Asad Ismi writes of J. Lawton Collins, President Eisenhower's special emissary to the Diem government. In 1954-55 Collins tried to extricate the U.S. from its commitment to Diem, but the maneuver was foiled by the intrepid Army Colonel Edward Lansdale, an executive of the Central Intelligence Agency.

One or the other of these essays will take most readers by surprise. People who were alert adults during our troop commitment in Viet Nam are certainly aware of Shoup and Gavin. The brass mavericks had a high profile. Gavin appeared on television. Shoup spoke at a junior college convention. They wrote articles in national magazines, and authored and edited widely-reviewed books. Though they did not join Vietnam Veterans Against the War or throw their medals away at Dewey Canyon III, the retired generals did take their anti-war views to the public in as determined a manner as possible while remaining within the bounds of establishment dissent. Those who followed the media at the time, but didn't read through the *Pentagon Papers,* will be interested to see that Gavin had expressed his judgement to the Joint Chiefs of Staff as part of his job, before the escalation of our troop commitment, and that many other military leaders gave voice to the same opinions, at work and in public.

Readers of my own thirtysomething generation, who didn't watch *Meet the Press* as children, and who came to history in the late 1970s and 1980s, will find it all new and exciting. We grew up during the formation of the revisionist consensus, the stab-in-the-back theory of widespread 20th century utility, which claims that the U.S. armed forces could have won the war in Viet Nam if only politicians had not hampered their efforts. The historian who appears in the press most often as the champion of this view is always introduced as *Colonel Harry Summers, who served in Viet Nam..*

Buzzanco strikes a strong blow against revisionism when he demonstrates that successful officers of World War II, who were privy to the best military information about Indochina, thought that our commitment to anti-communism in Viet Nam was a mistake, and went public with these views long before *Harry Summers, colonel of infantry* was negotiating the U.S. exit from Sai Gon. Buzzanco's documentation is the result of careful historical analysis, spanning archival research into primary sources, journalism, polemics, memoirs and professional literature. He demonstrates with industry and sophistication that it is not only hindsight to say that the U.S. military couldn't have won in Viet Nam. James Gavin and David Shoup said it before U.S. armed forces were ever committed to fighting a war in Southeast Asia..

Why did the U.S. government commit itself to protecting one shaky dictator after another in Viet Nam? Why did we venture, against professional counsel, to fight revolutionaries in the difficult terrain and among the hostile or indifferent peoples of a distant region, when mobilizing the American people for war was not an option in domestic politics or in the international balance of power?

It is impossible to point to a single event in the chain of cause and effect, action and reaction, which led to the U.S. government's decision to commit our military to a war in Viet Nam. But no matter how several and mixed the causes of that war, the history of our involvement was shaped, in certain moments, by a handful of players—moments that could have broken differently for millions of people.

Asad Ismi has found such a moment in 1954-55, when the U.S. bound itself to Ngo Dinh Diem. Ismi follows General J. Lawton Collins, U.S.A., as he arrives in Sai Gon in 1954, the representative of President Eisenhower, sent to find out what his nation should do. Ismi's dramaturgy has the seductiveness of inevitability and the heady promise of free choice. Collins was one of those WWII commanders with a nickname, a person to size up a situation and get things done. He had Ike's ear. He saw that the Republic of Viet Nam had no viable government, and he acted to cut the U.S. puppet strings. Collins failed when a junior officer working for another Executive agency forced the White House hand, but it was a close thing, a matter of cables crossing and orders delayed by a few hours, something Kipling would put in the mouth of an old boy at the officers' club. You should read the article. Don't wait for the movie.

Viet Nam Generation has not published a book of U.S. history of this kind before. We have tended to focus on social and intellectual history, rather than political and military history, mainly because we felt that the voices of social historians and cultural critics often go unheard. We have published articles and anthologies dealing with issues of race and gender, refugee communities, the G.I. resistance movement, and the antiwar movement. Even political historian Ben Kiernan's essay on the U.S. role in Cambodia, published in the first number of the first volume of *Vietnam Generation*,[1] focuses on the effects of U.S. bombardment on Khmer farmers. We feel that in addition to maintaining our committment to providing a forum for nontraditional and interdisciplinary scholarship, it's time to begin to seek out and publish the work of the bright young scholars who read on the U.S. war on Indochina and focus on military leaders and heads of state.

The Viet Nam war was waged a generation after World War II had expanded opportunity in higher education to many more Americans— the waltz of elites had simply become less convincing in the college classroom as an explanation of the world. Students who had grown up in the shadow of World War II and the collapse of European civilization as it either embraced or was destroyed by fascism, those whose parents had survived the Great Depression and the disappearance of western empire, no longer gave much credibility to the idea that there are responsible parties managing national and world affairs, whose success and failure can be traced by the expert for the edification of citizens. The Viet Nam war took place at a moment when communists around the world were urging poor people to take their fates into their own hands, and the U.S. was telling them the same thing.

But the war didn't just come along, it was brought about. Those of us who read combat narratives are often comfortable with the soldier's insistence that the war was beyond anyone's comprehension or control. We're also at home with the soldier's rumor, the weary activist's rant, that the whole thing was rigged, stage-managed by a secret few behind a charade of politics. All those stories are about being a victim, a tool or dupe. Who doesn't think of himself that way, outside of a very small sphere of family and work? Even the secret decision-makers probably consider themselves servants of the obvious path of interest.

Many of us are not at home with the idea of powerful men at large who are neither best understood as individuals acting out of personal history, nor as the simple agents of great forces. I squirm in embarrassment as I read *The Best and the Brightest* and *Bright Shining Lie*, because David Halberstam and Neil Sheehan so desperately want their parlor dramas to represent the fate of nations, so that the men they knew and held by the hand will seem as kings.[2] But these BosWash power journalists are right, there *were* men who made history for the rest of us. They didn't have an iron hand on events, and it's hard to accept that the pride or mania of one colonel or Cabinet destroyed Southeast Asia, but they and those like them were competing to manage, while most people just tried to cope.

It's hard to track someone like a general, a man acting with individual concerns, group standards, and mass power, while he's active. A wealthy intelligence agency will place enormous resources at the disposal of one expert who studies a single mid-level leader from a very important country for years and decades, and the conclusions reached still often aren't worth much. But time goes by and men die and capital shifts investment and documents become available and historians write more and more about events that power doesn't have the interest or the expertise to conceal any more, pointing up key issues that the news media is no longer confusing with distraction. The two articles of this journal issue are part of an effort to clear up the U.S. war on Southeast Asia by focusing on some generals, the men who were at work on a level between the palace and the paddy. Buzzanco and Ismi are young historians. We wish them long careers with many students and colleagues, and lengthy sabbaticals in the archives.

[1]   Ben Kiernan, "The American Bombardment of Kampuchea, 1969-1973," *Vietnam Generation* 1:1 (Winter 1989): 4-41.

[2]   David Halberstam, *The Best and the Brightest* 1969 (New York: Fawcett Crest) 1973; Neil Sheehan, *A Bright Shining Lie: John Paul Vann and America in Vietnam* (New York: Random House) 1988.

Division, Dilemma and Dissent: Military Recognition of the Peril of War in Viet Nam

Robert Buzzanco

> I believe that if we had and would keep our dirty, bloody, dollar-crooked fingers out of the business of these nations so full of depressed, exploited people, they will arrive at a solution of their own. That they design and want. That they fight and work for. [Not one] crammed down their throats by Americans.[1]

Thus former Marine Commandant General David Shoup attacked American participation in the Viet Nam war in early 1966. Such criticism from a respected military leader manifested an extraordinary yet relatively neglected aspect of the Viet Nam war. From the United States military's first consideration of policy toward Indochina after World War II until the reunification of Viet Nam a quarter-century later, the Joint Chiefs of Staff (JCS), respective service planners, and senior officers working in government—at different times and to varying degrees—questioned, criticized and even opposed America's war in Southeast Asia.

For the past decade various American military leaders have defended the U.S. military role in Viet Nam, claiming that weak politicians and public resistance prevented a certain military victory. While the war was in progress, however, American military leaders had no unified perspective on Viet Nam and were variously cautious, pessimistic, and divided over U.S. prospects in the war. Thus the military's current revisionism of Viet Nam can be challenged with evidence gathered from its own camp.[2]

Though the progression, over two decades, of military caution and criticism of involvement in Viet Nam is complex, certain themes emerge and demonstrate patterns of resistance. Military recognition of the peril of war in Viet Nam can be well demonstrated by studying three different cases of armed forces' criticism of involvement in Indochina. First, the U.S. military in the early 1950s opposed intervention in the First Indochina War and established the logic of military resistance to action in Viet Nam. Then, with American combat involvement in the war in the mid-1960s various service leaders recognized the political-military barriers to success. And finally, Generals Shoup, Matthew Ridgway, James Gavin, and others, provided a synthesis to military criticism of the war with their public attacks against U.S. involvement in Viet Nam from 1966 onward.

Grateful acknowledgement is given to the Lyndon B. Johnson Library for a grant which made it possible to complete this work.

In the early 1950s military leaders developed a critique of Viet Nam which would remain valid for two decades. Above all, the brass resisted war in Indochina because that area was not a priority in national security policy and because it understood the limits of American power. Accordingly, officers such as Air Force Chief of Staff Hoyt Vandenberg—concerned that French stability was the keystone to European security—warned in 1953 that the continued Franco-American commitment in Viet Nam might amount to "pouring money down a rathole." And in late 1954, after refusing to intervene during the Dien Bien Phu crisis, the JCS likewise maintained that support of the southern Vietnamese government "should be accomplished at low priority and not at the expense of other U.S. military programs and should not... impair the development... of effective and reliable allied forces elsewhere."[3]

Thus, the "Europe-centricity," to use George Mc.T. Kahin's term, of American military chiefs led them to preclude military action in Viet Nam. Ironically, U.S. political and diplomatic leaders who advocated assistance to and intervention in Indochina had similar "Europe first" premises, but where they believed that support of France in Viet Nam would serve as a q*uid pro quo* to ensure French fealty in NATO and maintain France's vital role in the reconstitution of the international Capitalist order, the military argued that Indochina was a risky diversion for France and NATO when problems in Europe were compelling. The brass, however, developed more specific reasons for their resistance to military involvement in Indochina, generally opposing war there because of their recognition of the destructive nature of French colonialism and indigenous sources of Vietnamese revolt; the strength and popular acceptance of Ho Chi Minh and the Viet Minh; the relationship between the Viet Minh and the People's Republic of China (PRC) and the threat of Chinese intervention; and the logistical and strategic problems which the U.S. would encounter in combat in Viet Nam.[4]

The U.S. military clearly understood that French imperialism had created an untenable political environment for native Vietnamese. Ho Chi Minh, leader of the indigenous Viet Minh independence movement, enjoyed the support of eighty percent of the Vietnamese, army planners estimated, yet eighty percent of these followers were not communists.[5] Even France's biggest booster in the military, Pacific Commander and later JCS Chair Admiral Arthur Radford, saw that "the French seem to have no popular backing from the local Indo-Chinese." Later the Joint Strategic Plans Committee defined the struggle in Viet Nam as "essentially an internal conflict." And by late 1954 Army analysts pointed out that the Viet Minh had grown to about 340,000 troops with about one-quarter *below* the seventeenth parallel.[6]

Military leaders also feared that intervention in Viet Nam could bring the PRC into the war as well. Thus in April 1952 the JCS warned against unduly provoking China, and a year later the Joint Strategic Survey Committee (JSSC) maintained that if France withdrew from Viet

Nam due to PRC pressure, the U.S. had no feasible military response. But Chair of the JCS (CJCS) Admiral Radford, testifying in executive session in February 1954, told the Senate Committee on Foreign Relations (SCFR) that Chinese support of the Viet Minh was not significant and in fact much less than American aid to France. Thus, regardless of whether military leaders believed that the Viet Minh or Chinese was America's biggest problem in Asia, they agreed that military support of the French in Indochina could be a huge cost to pay for the risks of a general war in Asia.[7]

Even without Chinese intervention an American military commitment to Viet Nam faced enormous barriers to success. In March 1950 Army intelligence recognized that Viet Nam's "rugged terrain" afforded great strategic advantages to the Viet Minh.[8] Air Force General Charles Cabell, director of the Joint Staff, also had a clear understanding of the hazards of combat in Viet Nam. "Terrain difficulties, the guerrilla nature of Viet Minh operations and the political apathy of the population," Cabell explained in 1953, "preclude decisive consolidation of areas cleared of Viet Minh, unless these areas are physically occupied by friendly forces. This commitment is beyond the capabilities of the friendly strength." In his debriefing in 1954 former Chief of the Military Assistance Advisory Group (MAAG), General Thomas Trapnell, cited the Viet Minh for its "clever war of attrition" and explained that Ho and Giap, believing that time and public opinion in France and the U.S. were on their side, would continue guerrilla operations. "A strictly military solution to the war," Trapnell explained, "is not possible."[9]

Other officers confirmed such bleak views. Admiral A.C. Davis, director of the Pentagon's Office of Military Assistance, concluded in early 1954 that military intervention in Viet Nam "had to be avoided at all costs." The Admiral warned that any American role would become massive— "one cannot go over Niagara Falls in a barrel only slightly," Davis mused—because "there is no cheap way to fight a war, once committed."[10] More importantly, Army Chief of Staff Matthew Ridgway successfully challenged advocates of intervention in the Spring of 1954. A military commitment in Viet Nam, Ridgway emphatically charged, "would constitute a dangerous strategic diversion of limited United States military capabilities and would commit our armed forces in a non-decisive theatre to the attainment of non-decisive local objectives." And Army Plans Chief General James Gavin in July echoed General Omar Bradley's warning about Korea when he observed that any U.S. guarantee to protect southern Viet Nam "involves the risk of embroiling [the] U.S. in the wrong war, in the wrong place, at the wrong time."[11]

Despite the military's strong reservations about involvement in Viet Nam from 1950 to 1954, the U.S. established a training mission to the nation it had ostensibly created at Geneva, the Republic of Viet Nam (RVN), and, as the military's leaders had warned, progressively escalated the American role in Viet Nam throughout the rest of the decade. Publicly

Viet Nam declined markedly as a foreign policy issue after 1955 but in the later 1950s Gavin, in *War and Peace in the Space Age*, and Ridgway in his memoirs criticized U.S. involvement in Indochina. Ridgway passionately opposed intervention in Viet Nam with words which were poignant yet empty

> When the day comes for me to face my Maker and account for my actions, the thing I would be most humbly proud of was the fact that I fought against, and perhaps contributed to preventing, the carrying out of some hare-brained tactical schemes which would have cost the lives of thousands of men. To that list of tragic accidents that fortunately never happened I would add the Indo-China intervention.[12]

By the early 1960s it was clear that Ridgway would have to change the script for his heavenly talk. Though America's military planners of the early 1950s had anticipated the serious if not insurmountable barriers to effective military action in Viet Nam Presidents John F. Kennedy and Lyndon B. Johnson progressively increased the U.S. commitment to the RVN and Johnson eventually deployed ground troops in early 1965.

Yet the situation which confronted the U.S. in Viet Nam in the early 1960s was less favorable than that during the 1950s. The French had been relieved to quit Indochina and other American allies were not eager to support military involvement in Viet Nam. The Viet Minh, France's enemy in the First Indochina War, was a shell compared to Ho's later forces comprised of the Viet Cong (VC), National Liberation Front (NLF), and Peoples Army of Viet Nam (PAVN). Within the U.S. McCarthyism and its corresponding anti-Communist obsession had waned, creating a political climate somewhat more conducive to noninvolvement. Internationally, America had to contend with matters more pressing than Southeast Asia: the Sino-Soviet split, the Berlin Wall, the Bay of Pigs, the Cuban missile crisis, and revolution in Africa, Latin America, and other parts of Asia. From 1961 to 1965 the U.S. thus had no compelling reason to intervene militarily in Viet Nam.

Nonetheless the U.S. did send combat troops to Da Nang in early 1965 to prevent an imminent RVN collapse and Communist victory. The armed forces leaders, especially appointees of Kennedy and Johnson, firmly supported the expanded American role in Indochina. At the same time, the generals charged with conducting the war recognized that political and military conditions in Viet Nam mitigated against American success. Even the stronger supporters of the war often had grave reservations about America's principally military approach to and prospects in Viet Nam, and their caution often moved beyond usual military doubts and differences of opinion on tactics and strategy to question the fundamental premises of U.S. policy in Viet Nam. Most importantly, the generals in the mid-1960s expressed caution, fear and worry over the inchoate political environment in the RVN: the commitment of combat forces and conventional war strategy; and the development of an effective pacification program.

From 1965 until the Tet Offensive in 1968 the U.S. directed its focus in Viet Nam toward military efforts. "Nevertheless," as General Douglas Kinnard observed in *The War Managers*, "there was always the realization that eventual stabilization of the country depended on... a viable government attuned to the needs of the Vietnamese people."[13] Indeed, the American military consistently recognized, on the heels of the autocratic Diem regime and the near-anarchic political situation created by a series of coups in 1964 and 1965, the need for a credible civilian government in the RVN and understood that continued political chaos would challenge if not shatter American prospects in the war.

Among Americans in Viet Nam few recognized the dangers of the internal political situation better than General Maxwell Taylor. Though ambassador to Saigon from July 1964 to July 1965, Taylor had served as Army Chief of Staff, military advisor to Kennedy, and Chair of the JCS. Thus throughout the Fall of 1964 he constantly warned that instability in the RVN was making military efforts untenable. In late November Taylor saw the U.S. playing "a losing game" in Viet Nam and found it "impossible to foresee a stable and effective government under any name in anything like the near future." At year's end the General observed that the war in southern Viet Nam was being waged on four fronts: "the Generals versus the government, the Generals versus the Ambassador, the Buddhists versus the government, and the Generals against the VC." Taylor understood, however, that the U.S. was limited in ways to pressure the RVN into adopting reforms. While he could look into "various degrees of controlling U.S. aid" and noted that "one possibility would be to go home," Taylor admitted that "we are not prepared to consider this."[14]

Simultaneously, officers in the Military Assistance Command, Viet Nam (MACV) recognized the deficiencies in the government of the RVN. Commander William Westmoreland in November 1964 scored the ineffective Vietnamese leadership and worried that earlier government reforms would be no "more than superficial or more than a lull in the storm." Westmoreland's Assistant Chief of Staff for Operations, General William Depuy, an ardent advocate of firepower and the strategy of attrition, nonetheless analyzed "the Revolutionary Spirit" in Viet Nam and observed that the RVN's leaders had not participated in the Viet Minh struggle against France and were thus viewed by the population-at-large as anti-nationalist collaborators. The RVN leaders, the Operations division added, were "petit bourgeoisie" while "the VC on the other hand prefer to mold their leaders from the common clay." The Vietnamese people did not support the government in the south, Depuy conceded, and American support of local politicians exacerbated tensions because the U.S. and its clients were "peculiarly vulnerable to VC propaganda and American endorsements of native leaders was a "kiss of death." Given such political circumstances, success depended on RVN reforms, which were "highly unlikely."[15]

By 1965 the deteriorating political conditions in the south were easily recognized. Taylor's "basic conclusion" was that the U.S. "is on a losing track in South Vietnam and must change course or suffer defeat, early or late as one chooses to interpret the known facts." Westmoreland likewise pessimistically envisioned within six months a Saigon government with strongholds only in provincial and district capitals, streets clogged with refugees, and a proliferation of Vietnamese "end the war" groups.[7] From such a scenario Westmoreland concluded that U.S. ground forces could stem the disintegration of the RVN and help create a stable government. The Marine deployments in Da Nang, however, did not assuage military caution about politics in the RVN.[16]

In June 1965 Westmoreland observed that religious and regional cleavages, the ineffectiveness of the Phan Huy Quat government, and growing frustration over two decades of war without victory in sight had created a "political crisis" in Viet Nam which threatened to erode the uncertain military situation even further. By late August, almost six months after ground troop commitments, the JCS was not sanguine about internal events in the south. The Chiefs recognized the VC's increasing capabilities, feared "the continued existence of a major Viet Cong infrastructure, both political and military, in the RVN," and lamented over "the lack of a viable politico/economic structure" in southern Viet Nam.[17] Army Chief of Staff Harold K. Johnson, during a crucial July 1965 meeting with the president and his advisors, was equally blunt, admitting that "we are in a face down. The solution, unfortunately, is long-term. Once the military problem is solved, the problem of political solution will be more difficult." Marine General Keith McCutcheon, Commander of the First Marine Air Wing (I MAW), thereafter explained that the southern economy had foundered since its "production base is under control of VC most of time," and added that the RVN could not establish as much-needed rationing system because "graft would undermine it."[18]

By the following Spring the RVN's political chaos had grown worse. New leader Nguyen Cao Ky and the Buddhists were at war, prompting McCutcheon to observe that "the political situation is really on the front burner and at times the temperature climbs to boiling." Amid another Buddhist crisis in the northern RVN, Maxwell Taylor complained that Prime Minister Ky "has had no success in placating or buying off his enemies." Ky, however, had shown "good judgment" in ᵉcting Buddhist calls for elections because the "political turmoil ʰ elections with their attendant factional struggles would generate" ⁿly contribute "to the detriment of the conduct of the war." "In ᵗ" Taylor lamented, "the Ky Government is in real danger as are ᵗerests." Taylor had thus clearly pointed out the American dilemma in Viet Nam. Despite repeated emphasis on creating a legitimate political structure in southern Viet Nam, the Ambassador admitted that popular elections would grievously destabilize the regime. Taylor's bleak analysis notwithstanding, his solution—increase military action—had already been proven wanting and offered little prospect of success.[19]

The Commanding General of the Marine's Pacific Fleet, General Victor Krulak, warned that continued turmoil in the south could create grave problems. "Repressive measures are all that is left" for the government to use to develop stability, Krulak feared, "and you will recall what happened after Diem launched his repressive measures." In a memo to Navy Undersecretary Robert Baldwin Krulak conceded that "despite all our public assertions to the contrary, the South Vietnamese are not—and never have been—a nation."[20]

The Army also expressed fear and frustration toward the RVN in its "Program for the Pacification and Long-Term Development of South Vietnam" (PROVN) study. Commissioned by Army Chief Harold K. Johnson in mid-1965 and released to MACV the following spring, the PROVN study urged the United States to use leverage against the RVN to enhance its political and military performance. Believing that the situation in Viet Nam had "seriously deteriorated," the Army Staff asserted that "1966 may well be the last chance to ensure eventual success." "Victory" could only be achieved by developing genuine support for the government among the peasants at the village, district, and provincial levels, where, the study concluded, "the war must be fought [and] won."[21] General Edward Lansdale, midwife to the Diem regime in the 1950s and advisor to presidents on Viet Nam thereafter, more pointedly observed that the "true struggle" in Viet Nam would be waged on a "political basis." The United States, however, had "too weak a political foundation" on its side. Lansdale compared the central government and constitution to "top layers of a foundation," but warned that "the vital bottom layers are missing."[22]

Despite such political uncertainty in the RVN the U.S. had deployed combat forces to Viet Nam in early 1965. American generals, however, questioned the necessity and efficacy of those troop commitments to Viet Nam and U.S. military strategy in the war. When American policymakers began to seriously consider sending combat troops into Viet Nam during the Kennedy presidency White House military advisor General Taylor and Pacific Commander Admiral Harry Felt, among others, balked because initial commitments, they believed, would escalate until American soldiers became fully engaged in hostilities in Viet Nam. David Shoup, Marine Commandant from 1959 to 1963, similarly asserted that the JCS discussed sending troops to Viet Nam frequently but "in every case... every senior officer that I knew... said we should never send ground combat forces into Southeast Asia." Such caution was still evident in September 1964, when MACV "did not contemplate" committing combat forces because, Taylor explained, Westmoreland thought that using American troops "would be a mistake, that it is the Vietnamese' war."[23]

Likewise a MACV study, in which Taylor concurred, completed just two months before Americans landed in Da Nang opposed introducing ground combat forces. The American advisory effort, Westmoreland and his staff observed, had shown diminishing returns and the U.S. had to pursue alternative approaches to the problems of Viet Nam. Accordingly, MACV considered the implications of various strategies and tactics in Viet Nam, including employing American forces in combat roles, but Westmoreland decided that any policy involving U.S. troops in battle carried great disadvantages: the U.S. would assume increasing combat responsibility, casualties would rapidly mount, and the northern Vietnamese would score propaganda victories by accusing the Americans of trying to control the country. Ground forces intervention, MACV and Taylor presciently understood, "would at best buy time and would lead to ever increasing commitments until, like the French, we would be occupying an essentially hostile foreign country." Thus the study recommended that the U.S. provide operational support and improve and adhere to its flawed advisory system.[24]

Just two months later the situation in Viet Nam had disintegrated further and MACV ignored its own strong reservations and best advice and requested combat troops, a plea which General Taylor "strongly opposed." But with the Army of the RVN (ARVN) suffering multiple defeats and the Rolling Thunder air campaign ineffective, President Johnson deployed two Marine battalions, which arrived in Da Nang on 8 March. Subsequently Westmoreland and Army Chief Johnson began to request additional troops, as Taylor had predicted, and the ambassador scored the military's "hasty and ill-conceived" proposals for a greater commitment.[25]

Even Chair General Earle Wheeler conceded in June that the U.S. combat presence in the RVN had made a negligible impact on the war and feared future VC offensives since those insurgents had yet to employ anywhere near their full capabilities. The ARVN meanwhile could not fight effectively and moreover had yet to reconstitute particularly-damaged units. Subsequently Wheeler and the other Chiefs urged a further expansion of American force strength in the RVN and intensified air attacks against the Democratic Republic of Viet Nam to stem Communist momentum in the south. Thus, six weeks prior to President Johnson's decision to increase the U.S. troop commitment to 125,000—less than the JCS wanted—Wheeler understood that Viet Nam was already an American war, a dilemma against which Westmoreland had warned at the beginning of the year. Marine Commandant Wallace Greene, during the July 1965 meetings leading to President Johnson's decision to escalate, added that the commitment would continue to grow. "How long will it take?" Greene pondered, "5 years—plus 500,000 troops. I think the U.S. people will back you," he optimistically concluded.[26] And in late August Wheeler admitted another problem facing his forces in Viet Nam, namely "the threat of CHICOM [Chinese Communist] intervention or aggression" in Southeast Asia or elsewhere in the western Pacific.[27]

Once committed, U.S. troops moved from static defense positions in Da Nang to active combat participation. Accordingly, American generals criticized the MACV war strategy. Attacking sanctuaries in or invading Cambodia or Laos—later championed by General Dave Richard Palmer and Colonel Harry Summers, among others—involved dangers recognized by the brass in the mid-1960s. In November 1964 Taylor saw "nothing but disadvantage in further stirring up the Cambodian border by implementing hot pursuit. We don't often catch the fleeing VC in the heart of SVN; I see little likelihood of doing better in Cambodia." In 1966 General Max Johnson—former Planning Officer for the JCS and Commandant of the Army War College, and then military analyst for U.S. *News and World Report*—dismissed advocates of establishing a cordon-zone defense across Viet Nam and into Laos (Westmoreland's unconsummated 1966 El Paso Plan) because such a military push from the Demilitarized Zone (DMZ) across the Laotian panhandle to the Thai border would involve about 400,000 troops and an unspecified but "enormous" logistical increase, but it would not ensure safety against the elusive VC.[28]

General Johnson also criticized advocates of a ground offensive into the DRVN, which General Dave Palmer believed was a "sure route" to victory. To Johnson an invasion of the north either across the DMZ or through an amphibious landing at Hai Phong might "require 12 U.S. divisions just to subdue the delta," and could neither be kept secret nor achieve tactical surprise. Though some war leaders complained of "one hand tied behind their back," Johnson concluded (optimistically) that the military had to realize that attempting to achieve a victory in Viet Nam could "take at least 10 to 12 divisions, a huge increase in air power or both. Where the U.S. now has about 190,000 men in Vietnam, upward of 500,000 might be needed."[29]

General Edward Lansdale lashed out against MACV's strategy of attrition and its gauge of progress, the body count. Lansdale lamented that "we concentrate on eliminating the enemy by physical means and have relied superstitiously on the magic of casualty numbers to reassure ourselves that we are winning, since the enemy's casualties are far heavier than ours; Yet the enemy has steadily increased the size of his forces in South Viet Nam." Likewise, then-Colonel Dave Richard Palmer had written in a West Point text that "attrition is not a strategy.... A commander who resorts to attrition admits his failure to conceive of an alternative.... He uses blood in lieu of brains." To Palmer the employment of attrition thus offered "hard truth" that the U.S. "was strategically bankrupt in Vietnam."[30]

Even Westmoreland, the architect of the strategy of attrition, recognized the tenuous nature of his policy. In public he claimed that the U.S. was winning its war of attrition and might begin withdrawing troops by 1968 or 1969. But "killing guerrillas," the Commander briefed President Johnson in Guam in 1967, "is like killing termites with a screw driver, where you have to kill them one by one and they're inclined to multiply as rapidly as you kill them." Consequently, when General Kinnard surveyed U.S. Generals who had served in Viet Nam he found that forty-two percent believed that large-scale operations had been overdone from the beginning, that fifty-five percent considered the kill ratio a misleading measure of performance, and that 61 percent admitted inflating the body count. "The immensity of the false reporting" of casualty numbers, one General remarked, "is a blot on the honor of the army."[31]

Such frustration, pessimism and anger was pervasive within the military. Upon returning from a trip to Viet Nam in November 1967 Vice-President Hubert Humphrey reported that he had asked MACV's officers to estimate how much longer the war would continue but "encountered no prophets." After the 1968 Tet Offensive, which many Generals claimed was a military victory but a psychological defeat, Westmoreland nonetheless recognized that "we are in a whole new ball game where we face a determined, highly disciplined enemy, fully mobilized to achieve a quick victory." General Wheeler reported subsequently that the VC had the "will and capability to continue" and that Communist "determination appears to be unshaken." Wheeler moreover noted that VC attacks had created significant problems in all four tactical war zones, had greatly reduced the effectiveness of the GVN, caused the pacification program to suffer a "severe set back," and created a flood of refugees. Though MACV and Wheeler may have later interpreted Tet as a decisive military victory, the Chair of JCS had concluded in late February 1968, "in short, it was a very near thing."[32] Harold K. Johnson was more blunt. "We suffered a loss," he wrote to Westmoreland, "there can be no doubt about it."[33]

Along with the armed services' concerns over political turmoil in the RVN and the combat role of American forces in Viet Nam came a divisive conflict within MACV over the nature and importance of the U.S. pacification program. From earlier formations on policy in Viet Nam it was clear that the military envisioned limiting U.S. forces to a support role for the ARVN. In 1962 MAAG Chief General Lionel McGarr explained that the U.S., "in providing the GVN the tools to do the job... must not offer so much that they forget that the job of saving the country is theirs— only they can do it." Accordingly the strategy of pacification, also called counterinsurgency (CI), was to be the means by which the RVN and U.S. would quash the VC insurgency. Pacification, military analysts hoped, would entail American support personnel pacifying the VC threat on the local level and thus free the ARVN to conduct military operations.[34] As

General William P. Yarborough, head of the Army's Special Warfare Center at Fort Bragg, explained, "the entire conflict... is 80 percent in the realm of ideas and only 20 percent in the field of physical conflict." Nonetheless, within a few years the conflict over the pacification program would demonstrate military criticism of and confusion over the war and spark an intense interservice battle.[35]

After America's substantive commitment to the RVN after the Gulf of Tonkin resolution in August 1964, it was clear that the VC held the military and political initiative in southern Viet Nam. In late 1964 Westmoreland admitted that the pacification program had "regressed," and he complained that "it is no good congratulating ourselves on the progress in one sector [some improvements in the ARVN] when the campaign as a whole is not going well." And in late February 1965 the Commander conceded that pacification was "virtually halted" and feared a breakdown in the RVN within six months.[36]

Westmoreland, however, preferred conventional operations to pacification, while Taylor and the Marines argued that the U.S. should emphasize CI. In mid-April Taylor complained that MACV was relying on heavy weapons which were "inappropriate for counterinsurgency operations." General Krulak asserted that a successful strategy in Viet Nam "must embrace economic, political, sociological and religious programs" as well as the military effort. "No military strategy, however sound," Krulak believed, "will achieve success without corresponding non-military progress" to bring stability to the Vietnamese.[37]

In its PROVN study of 1966 the Army Staff, contrary to Westmoreland's convictions, had reached similar conclusions. The PROVN authors advocated that the MACV pressure the RVN into developing an effective pacification program. Rural Construction, as the Army referred to CI, should constitute America's principal effort in Viet Nam; "it must be designated unequivocally," the study explained, "as the major US/GVN effort. It will require the commitment of a preponderance of RVNAF [RVN Armed Forces] and GVN paramilitary forces, together with adequate U.S. support and coordination and assistance." The MACV, however, would not waver from its strategy of attrition and so paid lip service to and ultimately shelved the PROVN report. But Krulak again urged that CI be emphasized, lamenting that the VC, despite suffering heavy casualties, were tying down American units in big-unit fire fights and diverting U.S. forces away from the village level. Thus the Marine General was "deeply concerned that the enemy has played the tune, & induced us to dance to it."[38]

Not surprisingly, Marine Commandant Wallace Greene publicly championed the pacification program. In 1966 Greene asserted that "I think the victory will hinge on the success of the pacification program." The Commandant, at the same time the Wheeler stated that the U.S. mission was "to kill as many Viet Cong" as possible and to "destroy" areas used by the VC, told the Senate Armed Services Committee that "we aren't executing this program by the rifle and the sword. We are helping these people help themselves." The U.S. and ARVN "could kill every Vietcong and North Vietnamese in South Vietnam," Greene warned, "and still lose the war."[39] Even Wheeler, despite his public advocacy of firepower, warned Westmoreland that continued failure to show progress on CI—along with ARVN passivity—would cause increased problems for the MACV staff from U.S. political leaders.[40]

The debate over pacification also helped fuel an intense interservice conflict. After reading that the Army had criticized the Marines' "beach head mentality," General Krulak complained that "there has been an artesian flow of anti-Marine sentiment bubbling from General Larsen [Stanley Larsen, a MACV deputy] since the early days of our military involvement in Vietnam." Marine Aviation Commander General Norman Anderson similarly charged that MACV—despite pleas that logistical problems caused by the influx of new troops after Tet had become "almost too great to comprehend"—had ignored the Marines. "The four stars in Saigon merely wave their hands and release dispatches for directing the units to move," Anderson complained. "I think much of it is by design, with the ultimate aim of embarrassing the III MAF [3d Marine Amphibious Force]." And Krulak, after publication of an article in the Los Angeles Times had detailed Army criticism of the Marine performance in Viet Nam, publicly criticized the paper but charged that "the attack—one of several—was launched by the army, of course. Westmoreland, Abrams and a character named Larsen." Were it possible, Krulak noted, he would publish a rejoinder titled, "The Army Is At It Again."[41]

Such interservice confusion and division was indicative of America's military experience in Viet Nam. The armed forces at no time possessed unity of purpose, did not similarly understand the nature of the war, never agreed upon an effective, uniform strategy, and always recognized the dangers and barriers to success inherent in military involvement in the Viet Nam war. The war managers were aware that without a stable government in the south, success would be illusory or temporary, that it was infeasible if not impossible to save a geographic entity that was not a nation. Yet they supported the war. Different officers understood throughout the early 1960s that the Vietnamese would have to bear responsibility for their security, but in 1965 the U.S. became inextricably involved in a war of attrition, and thereafter Americanized the conflict until the U.S. commitment reached massive, and tragic proportion. And by the later 1960s many Generals admitted that the services were fighting each other with more vigor than against the enemy. General Bruce Palmer, Westmoreland's Army Deputy in Viet Nam, suggests that the JCS recognized in the mid-1960s that U.S. strategy would fail, yet did not inform civilian leaders of their pessimism. Accordingly, in General Kinnard's 1976 survey, 53 percent of the war leaders contended that America should not have been involved in combat in Viet Nam.[42]

Clearly American military leaders understood the severity of their problems in the Viet Nam war. Despite their support of the war, the Generals' internal criticisms, suggested alternatives, and battles against each other reflected on a confused, divided and cautious military which conducted the Viet Nam war. General Lansdale came to terms with the dilemma of Viet Nam better than most brass. "In all this immense activity," the self-proclaimed savant and agent *provocateur* of Viet Nam conceded in a 1968 article in *Foreign Affairs*, "we seem to be struggling toward some day when the long war will end with a whisper instead of a bang. The whisper is apt to be a prolonged one." Other generals, like Lansdale, also recognized that America would ultimately fail in Viet Nam, but they subordinated their doubts, reluctance, and alarm about the war due to self-delusion, acquiescence to the political will, or as General Shoup later charged, because of the opportunities the war offered to advance their careers.[43]

It seems likely, however, that the U.S. military developed its policies on Viet Nam with a strong sense of politics in mind as well. Given various important generals' consistent recognition of the peril of involvement in Indochina and their repeated access to information on the perilous nature of the war, it appears that the military understood that it would not succeed in Viet Nam. Rather than finding a way out of the tragedy which Viet Nam had become, however, American service leaders seemed more concerned with deflecting political responsibility for the American failure onto civilian leaders who, many generals would later charge, had made U.S. troops fight with "one hand tied behind their back."

In fact, from the earlier 1960s on, the military understood that the Johnson White House would not commit unlimited resources— troops or bombs—to the war in Viet Nam.[44] Thus Westmoreland and others repeatedly called for more troops, activation of reserves and wholly unrestrained air strikes against the DRVN, but understood that such authorization would not be forthcoming from Washington nor would it likely alter the inexorable deterioration of the U.S. position in the war. Yet rather than confronting the dilemma of Viet Nam and seeking a less violent solution, the military essentially recycled its requests for escalation in order to force the president to turn them down and thus bear responsibility for the continued failure in the war. Given Johnson's vacillating approach to the war and his refusal to introspectively contemplate the growing tragedy of Viet Nam, the president and MACV leadership might have deserved the political games they played against each other had not millions of lives hung in the balance.[45]

U.S. military leaders recognized early in the war that the White House was anxious over the size and nature of its commitment to Viet Nam. In December 1965 Westmoreland told Ambassador Henry Cabot Lodge that he might request extended terms of enlistment and an activation of reserves for Viet Nam, but he knew that such an authorization "might require some drastic action that could be politically difficult for the President." In early 1967 the MACV Commander also recognized that various factors—enemy elusiveness, intelligence shortcomings, helicopter support, troop availability—had mitigated against U.S. efforts and Westmoreland had to "say without hesitation... [that] the ground war cannot be significantly accelerated beyond the current pace."[46]

Just weeks later, after Westmoreland had reported enormous increases in enemy-initiated military action, Wheeler ordered the data suppressed because "if these figures should reach the public domain, they would, literally, blow the lid off of Washington." Only months later the JCS and the MACV—clearly aware of Washington's reluctance to dramatically expand the war—expected the Pentagon to "avoid the explosive congressional debate and U.S. reserve call-up implicit in" Westmoreland's latest reinforcement request. That autumn the President himself made clear his view of the military's recommendations on policy, ordering Harold K. Johnson to tell the JCS to "search for imaginative ideas to... bring this war to a conclusion." The armed services leadership, Johnson told the Army Chief, should not "just recommend more men or that we drop the Atom bomb" since the President himself "could think of those ideas."[47]

Only months later, however, the military entirely dismissed the President's orders. The greatest crisis of the war, the enemy's Tet Offensive, would lay bare the vacuous nature of U.S. military policy and lead to a political showdown which has reverberated through American foreign policy considerations to this day.[48] Despite later claims of decisive success, military reports in February and March 1968 were bleak and pessimistic and often alarmist.[49] Nonetheless, Westmoreland and Wheeler—at the very time that the White House, congress, media and American public had been unnerved if not shocked by Tet—requested 206,000 more troops and the activation of 280,000 reservists.[20] Under the best circumstances, White House approval of such an immense request was hardly likely. Given the crisis atmosphere which Tet had created, such reinforcement was simply not possible— and U.S. military leaders understood that.[50]

On 9 February, two weeks prior to his visit to Saigon which would result in a grim assessment of the situation in Viet Nam, Wheeler already feared that the MACV's immediate needs "could very well be jeopardized by adding... longer range requirements at this time." The Chiefs, Wheeler told Westmoreland, "can handle only one major problem at a time," and submitting proposals for any major new program could "derail any urgent requirements you may now be thinking about submitting." Similarly, Harold K. Johnson spent a "grueling day on the hill" on 17 February discussing extending terms of service in Viet Nam but, he cabled back to Bruce Palmer, one of Westmoreland's deputies, it was an "exceptionally sensitive" issue which the Army Chief "doubt[ed]... would receive favorable consideration." Indeed, when Johnson told lawmakers that a redeployment of the 82d Airborne Division might require longer tours in Viet Nam "my observation was dismissed out of hand."[51]

A week later, while Wheeler was in Viet Nam but prior to submitting the request for 206,000 troops to Washington, Bruce Palmer told Westmoreland that Dwight Beach, the Army's Pacific Commander, had learned of the reinforcement plan and "had commented that it would shock them [Washington officials]." At the same time, as Neil Sheehan reports, Ambassador Ellsworth Bunker tried to dissuade Westmoreland from asking for such enormous numbers of troops, warning that reinforcement was "politically impossible" even if the President had wanted to escalate, which was also more unlikely than ever.[52] Westmoreland himself later admitted that he and Wheeler "both knew the grave political and economic implication of a major call-up of reserves." But the MACV Commander also suspected that even the JCS Chair was "imbued with the aura of crisis" in Washington and had thus dismissed the MACV's sanguine outlook on the war.[53]

In any event, it seems clear that the principal U.S. military and political leaders in February 1968 recognized that the war had changed dramatically, that success was more remote than ever, and that any significant escalation was impossible. Nonetheless, the reinforcement request forced the President to confront his policies in Viet Nam, reject any future escalation, withdraw from the 1968 campaign, and bear the burden for the war. Since then, military leaders have continued to successfully exploit their interpretations of Tet and of the war itself— military success in the field undermined by craven politicians, the media, and the antiwar movement at home—to rehabilitate American intervention in Viet Nam and create the conditions for intervention in Latin America and the Persian Gulf.[54]

At the same time that Westmoreland and others were trying to transfer responsibility for the American failure onto political and media figures, General Shoup, Ridgway, Gavin and others were directly and intensely criticizing the war. Beginning in 1966, when support for the war was still strong, until U.S. withdrawal, the generals broke ranks with military tradition by publicly condemning American involvement in Viet Nam and urging immediate disengagement. In their arguments against the war these generals provided a synthesis to the opposition of the brass in the 1950s and reservations of the war leaders of the 1960s. By the 1970s retired antiwar officers had given definition to earlier military doubts and warnings about Viet Nam and developed a complete and cogent indictment against the war. Above all, Shoup, Ridgway and Gavin believed that the war in Viet Nam damaged the national interest. More specifically, these brass critics determined that the anti-Communist political assumptions which had prompted American intervention were faulty; that U.S. military strategy would inevitably fail; and the economic and moral consequences of the war would be long-lived.[55]

The U.S. military commitment to Viet Nam, the brass charged, did not serve the national interest. In 1966 Shoup doubted whether "the whole of South East Asia... is worth the life or limb of a single American." Ridgway added that America's imprecise and tenuous mission in Viet Nam did not "harmonize with our national interests," while in 1970 he observed that the war was undermining American hopes for arms control, exacerbating U.S.-Soviet tension, causing excessively heavy casualties, and draining the nation's capacity to react to crises elsewhere. "There is a limit to our power," Ridgway wrote to George McGovern in 1972, "notwithstanding the arrogant cynicism of those in our society who still cling to the false premises that we are superior to other peoples and that our industrial might could be marshalled in time to defeat any enemy who might attack us. Certainly we cannot be the world's policeman." General Gavin similarly ridiculed President Nixon's claim that he would not be the "first president to lose a war" or to besmirch the national honor. America's reputation, Gavin believed, could not be destroyed after almost 200 years. Thus the "national honor" was not at stake in Viet Nam; "it is common sense."[56]

Like the officers of the 1950s and the war leaders of the 1960s the generals criticized internal politics in the RVN and challenged the political assumptions which had prompted U.S. intervention in Viet Nam. In 1967 Gavin, appearing on *Meet the Press*, feared continued political turmoil in Viet Nam. "If we do not have stability in the government [RVN], it is all lost," he warned. Shoup more critically added that the leaders of the RVN were less popular among southern Vietnamese than Ho and the Communists. Accordingly he described the war as a struggle between "those crooks in Saigon" and Vietnamese nationals seeking a better life. The former Commandant also charged that America's enemy was "99 percent South Vietnamese" and that the United States had actually intervened in a civil war.

Shoup also attacked America's obsession with anti-Communism. Viet Nam, Shoup believed, was not the place to make a stand against the international Left. "It's about 8000 miles over the water," he explained, "I don't think we have a record of but two people walking on water and one of them failed. They don't have enough ships in the next X years, or enough airplanes to get over here. I don't know what they're going to get here with."[57] Gavin meanwhile believed that U.S. policy in Viet Nam was in fact "serving Communist interests perfectly" by freeing the PRC and Soviet Union to meddle elsewhere and by focusing American attention on Indochina when other areas, such as Europe or the Middle East, were more critical to national security. General Gavin also found it ironic that while the U.S. feared a world-wide Communist conspiracy, Soviet leader Nikita Khrushchev had withdrawn from Cuba in 1962 while "those who urge the United States to sharply increase its power in Vietnam demonstrate that the Soviets are more flexible in their foreign policy than we are."[58]

Despite the generals' criticism, anti-Communism had helped fuel American intervention into Viet Nam. Consequently the antiwar military leaders argued that U.S. strategy would certainly fail. Gavin explained that America, because it had not established goals or requirements in Viet Nam, could only react to Communist initiatives. Conditions in Viet Nam in 1965, the General believed, were "not essentially different" than in 1954. Saigon, vulnerable to sabotage and insurgency, and Hanoi, exposed to air attacks, were mutual hostages. Thus, Gavin maintained that military victory against the DRVN was not feasible and that American concern with Viet Nam had grown "alarmingly out of balance." Ridgway added that America's stated political goals had been "numerous, tenuous, and by no means clearly within the zone of U.S. vital interests, while the military objectives... tend to run away with the political."[59]

Even worse, General Gavin believed, was America's consistent military escalation in Viet Nam. After returning from Viet Nam in late 1967 Gavin appeared on *Meet the Press* and argued that U.S. troop levels should be frozen at 250,000 and that ARVN troops should immediately begin to take over the war. The General added that the U.S. should maintain a unilateral cease fire and cease ground combat operations as well. "I would certainly stop all escalation," Gavin stressed, "and as soon as we could, begin to bring troops out." Escalation moreover undermined U.S. claims that it was fighting a limited war in Viet Nam. Shoup was certain that the American commitment would continue to expand; "you can just pull any figure [number of troops] out of the hat and that would not be enough," he feared. America's use of combat power, Marine Colonel James Donovan likewise charged, was never flexible or limited. "It has been massive," he charged.[60]

Though too intense to qualify as limited, the U.S. could not considerably expand its military efforts, Shoup and Gavin explained, because the PRC could intervene with troops of its own in response to American escalation. By 1966 Gavin was "quite uneasy about an [American] overresponse in Vietnam" which could provoke Mao to intervene. In 1970 he rejected suggestions that the U.S. conduct military operations north of the DMZ or in Laos or Cambodia because Chinese retaliation would be "absolutely catastrophic in its implications." Gavin also urged that the U.S. recognize the PRC and accept its entry into the United Nations. Isolating China, the General concluded, only led to greater, if not irreconcilable, conflicts.[61]

Gavin even proposed an alternative strategy to avoid undue escalation or a widened war. American military planners, Gavin advised in a well-publicized article in *Harper's Magazine* and in testimony at the nationally televised "Vietnam Hearings" of the SCFR in early 1966, should pull back U.S. forces from the interior to a series of coastal enclaves along the eastern shore of the RVN, particularly at Da Nang and Cam Ranh Bay. American troops would hold the enclaves, patrol and support the ARVN, and eventually entrust security responsibility to the Vietnamese themselves.[62]

Gavin's proposal attracted great attention. Ridgway, General Anthony McAuliffe, Walter Lippman, and Senators Joseph Clark, J. William Fulbright, Mike Mansfield, George Aiken, and George McGovern, among others, endorsed the enclaves plan. Administration representatives, however, rejected Gavin's idea. Secretary of Defense Robert McNamara, Ambassador to Saigon Henry Cabot Lodge, and Undersecretary of State George Ball criticized the enclaves proposal. Commander Westmoreland charged that a retreat to enclaves would imply that the U.S. had conceded defeat in Viet Nam. General Taylor also criticized Gavin's plan, publicly asserting that a pull-back to enclaves would lead to a "crushing defeat of international proportions." But in 1964 and 1965 Taylor had privately advocated a coastal enclave mission as the best way to get American troops engaged in the war at relatively low risk until the ARVN could take responsibility for the war. Taylor's inconsistency notwithstanding, Gavin had presented the United States with an option to temper its involvement in Viet Nam which had received widespread support, but also one which civilian and military officials conducting the war had ignored or rejected.[63]

Perhaps more important than their strategic evaluations, the Generals condemned the Viet Nam war on moral and economic grounds as well. In 1966 Shoup attacked both the war and domestic problems, admonishing college students to be more concerned with issues of greater urgency than Communism—including racism, political corruption, and corporate irresponsibility. Ridgway similarly criticized America's air war in Viet Nam, finding "nothing in the present situation... that requires us to bomb a small Asian nation 'back to the stone age,'" and observing that the use of nuclear weapons in Viet Nam would constitute the "ultimate in immorality."[64]

In 1967 General Hugh Hester more stridently scored America's "brutal, cruel, and disgraceful war" and later insisted that the U.S. had to quit Viet Nam and confront "poverty, ignorance and bigotry at home." Ridgway noted that the U.S. could eventually court financial ruin by diverting resources to Viet Nam, where no returns could be expected. Marine General John Bouker resigned because American "policies of genocide in Vietnam and suppression of the individual at home have alienated me completely" from the United States. And Shoup, appearing before the SCFR in 1971, was distressed that Viet Nam was still a burning issue. "Most depressing it is," he lamented, "that... there have been a continued killing and maiming of men, women and children, destruction of villages, crops, woodlands, and countryside in South Vietnam and much, much more of the same in two additional countries that have been invaded."[65]

With such criticism Shoup, Ridgway and Gavin made a significant contribution to the national debate on Viet Nam. Because of their experience as military leaders the antiwar brass had a level of credibility which few could match and they could not be dismissed by the mainstream media or politicians. Accordingly, their dissent was well-publicized. They wrote books and articles, appeared before congressional committees, and often made the front page of major newspapers. Gavin, in fact, considered running for President in 1968. The general, a lifelong Democrat who bolted the party to protest Lyndon Johnson's conduct of the war, feared that the Republicans would nominate someone as hawkish as the incumbent. "It cannot be a Reagan," Gavin warned, "a most attractive man but facing firmly toward the past." The military critics also had an important role in the development of the chain of opposition to the war. Journalists and politicians often cited the brass' criticism to legitimate their own dissent, and in turn more Americans began to question the war and participate in the peace movement. Gavin, in fact, applauded the antiwar forces, finding that the "militant, dissident youth... are the only real hope for our country." Dr. Benjamin Spock offered a slightly different opinion. The dissent of one General, he wrote to Hugh Hester, was "easily worth the objections of ten professors or ministers."[66]

If Spock's formula was valid then American generals did indeed constitute a strong force against the Viet Nam war. While Ridgway, Gavin, and Shoup were exceptional among military figures in that they openly attacked the war, they were not alone in criticizing U.S. involvement in Viet Nam. Gavin maintained that most younger officers agreed with him in the late 1960s, and Shoup added that a great many military leaders did not support "what we have done or what we are now doing" in Viet Nam. General J. Lawton Collins likewise added that he did not "know of a single senior commander that [sic] was in favor of fighting on the land mass of Asia."[67] Indeed, from 1950 to the 1970s American military leaders often did not support U.S. policy in Indochina. Throughout over two decades of war American Generals recognized that the U.S. had made fundamental and egregious errors in Viet Nam: despite a constantly-unstable political structure the U.S. continued its military commitment to various governments in the RVN; the U.S. lacked a coherent and viable military strategy; and involvement in the war damaged American welfare at home and its influence abroad and caused seemingly interminable anguish in both the U.S. and Viet Nam.

The armed services had an ambivalent role in causing such destruction and suffering. Though a good many generals advocated the American commitment to Viet Nam and the use of intensive firepower while the war was fought, a considerable number of military leaders were cautious, doubtful of success, or opposed to U.S. involvement in Indochina. In the 1950s the military, led by Generals Collins and Ridgway, had resisted advocates of intervention and opposed expanding the American commitment to the RVN after the 1954 Geneva Conference.

In the mid-1960s many generals believed that the U.S. had legitimate reasons to stake its prestige and national treasure on the survival of the RVN, yet they also criticized, often virulently, and questioned whether America's principally and intensive military approach to the war—and the attendant costs in men and material—could achieve success. By the later 1960s Shoup, Ridgway, Gavin and other brass had assailed the American role in the war and developed a scathing critique of U.S. foreign policy. They understood, as General Lansdale put it, that "the Communists have let loose a revolutionary idea in Vietnam and it will not die by being... bombed, or smothered by us."[68] Though not pacifists or partisans of the New Left, the anti-Viet Nam war generals were pragmatic and conscientious objectors to the extended Cold War and increasingly hot war in Southeast Asia.

Collectively, the Generals who were cautious about or opposed to American involvement in Indochina over the course of two decades can make valuable contributions to the historical record of the Viet Nam war. While many conservative revisionists now argue that the U.S. failed in Viet Nam because of craven politicians or public opposition, the Generals' repeated dissent suggests that America suffered a military defeat. Since the early 1950s, military leaders had warned of the potentially disastrous consequences of war in Viet Nam, yet America continued to support the RVN and rushed into war in the mid-1960s and consequently proved much of the analysis on Viet Nam of the previous decade's military brass to be correct.

Throughout the war, U.S. military leaders always had access to information on the shortcomings of the American effort, deficiencies in the RVN's military and political establishments, and the strengths of the enemy. Accordingly, the MACV leadership developed its policies for Viet Nam in a constant atmosphere of crisis and out of acknowledged weakness. Yet the military never exhibited the political courage or institutional integrity to fundamentally confront its dilemma in Viet Nam. Instead, U.S. generals—in the 1960s and since then—have blamed external forces such as Dove legislators, the media or protesting college students for a failure which was militarily unavoidable under any circumstances.

Of course the military's postwar revisionism is disingenuous as well. Westmoreland himself admitted in 1969 that Lyndon Johnson—though he used force with more restraint than the MACV Commander would have preferred—did not tell him how to run the war. "I, in effect, had a carte blanche in the devising and pursuing [of] tactics and the battlefield strategy of the war," he pointed out.[69] What Westmoreland and others did not acknowledge was that the military had no homogenous or consensus outlook on the war. Many generals, internally divided over both politics and strategy, recognized that military success was uncertain if not unlikely. In short, many service leaders—some ten or twenty years prior to American withdrawal from Viet Nam in 1975—simply understood that the war would not be won.

Military dissent with regard to Viet Nam also demonstrated that American leaders had legitimate choices other than their massive commitment to the RVN. Indeed, with so many officers questioning American involvement in Viet Nam it is clear that the war could have been avoided on military grounds. Many generals, rather than being naive or unduly optimistic, had realistically evaluated the peril involved in a military campaign in Indochina. They had nonetheless ignored their own frequently bleak analyses with the full complicity of the civilian policymaking establishment. Rather than reappraise strategy and the war itself, American leaders deluded themselves that future success was possible, or at least hoped that they could avoid responsibility for the imminent disaster. A black wall with 58,000 names on it and an Asian nation destroyed beyond feasible reconstruction suggest otherwise.

In a failed and tragic foreign and military policy episode, however, those generals who questioned, criticized or resisted the war stand out at positive examples. Doubting from the beginning the viability of American intervention into Vietnamese affairs many officers conducted an offensive against U.S. military involvement in Indochina, and over the course of two decades other armed forces leaders provided reinforcement. Perhaps a greater awareness of their dissent might help to prevent such mistakes in the future. But it is also worth considering Matthew Ridgway's version of discussion with Secretary of State Dean Rusk shortly after Lyndon Johnson had committed combat troops to Viet Nam in early 1965: "'My God Dean,' Ridgeway exclaimed, 'Don't we ever learn anything.' There was no answer."[70]

[1] Shoup speech at Junior College World Affairs Day, Los Angeles, 14 May 1966, reprinted in U.S. Congress, Senate, Committee on Foreign Relations, *Present Situation in Vietnam*, 90th Cong., 2d Sess., 1968: 47.

[2] On conservative revisionism of Viet Nam see Walter LaFeber, "The Last War, the Next War, and the New Revisionists," *democracy* 1 (1981): 93-103; George Herring, "America and Vietnam: The Debate Continues," *American Historical Review* 92:2 (April 1987): 350-62; Bob Buzzanco, "The American Military's Rationale Against the Vietnam War," *Political Science Quarterly* 101:4 (Winter 1986): 559-76.

[3] "Substance of Discussions at State-JCS Meeting at Pentagon," 24 Apr 1953, United States, Department of State, *Foreign Relations of the United States*, 1952-54, vol. 13, part 1: 496-503 [hereafter cited as *FRUS* with appropriate year, volume, and page numbers]; JCS memo for Secretary of Defense, "Additional Aid to Indochina," 9 Oct 1953, Record Group 330, Records of the Office of Assistant Secretary of Defense for International Security Affairs, and the Office of Military Assistance, CD 091.3, Indochina, 1953 [hereafter cited as RG 330 with appropriate filing designation]; JCS memo for Secretary of Defense, "Retention and Development of Forces in Indochina," 22 Sep 1954, Record Group 218, Records

of the Joint Chiefs of Staff, CCS 092, Asia (6-25-48), section 83 [hereafter cited as RG 218 with appropriate filing designation]. For a full development of the military's opposition to intervention in Viet Nam in the early 1950s see my "Prologue to Tragedy: U.S. Military Opposition to intervention in Vietnam, 1950-1954," to be published in *Diplomatic History* 16 (1992).

4   George Mc.T. Kahin, "The United States and the Anticolonial Revolutions in Southeast Asia, 1945-1950," in Yonosuke Nagai and Akira Iriye, eds., *The Origins of the Cold War in Asia* (New York) 1977: 338-61; On "Europe first" views of diplomatic establishment and the restoration of French control in Indochina see also George Herring, "The Truman Administration and the Restoration of French Sovereignty in Indochina," *Diplomatic History* 1 (Spring 1977): 97-117; Walter LaFeber, "Roosevelt, Churchill, and Indochina: 1942-1945," *American Historical Review* 80 (Dec 1985): 1277-1295; Christopher Thorne, "Indochina and Anglo-American Relations, 1942-1945," *Pacific Historical Review* 45 (Feb 1976): 73-96; Gary Hess, "Franklin Roosevelt and Indochina," *Journal of American History* 59 (Sep 1972): 353-368; Gary Hess, "The First American Commitment in Indochina: The Acceptance of the 'Bao Dai Solution,' 1950," *Diplomatic History* 2 (Fall 1978): 331-350.

5   Army P&O Report on "U.S. Position with Respect to Indochina," 25 Feb 1950, Record Group 319, Records of the Army Staff, Plans and Operations Division, G-3, 091, Indochina TS [hereafter cited as RG 319 with appropriate filing designation].

6   JCS 1992/22, "Estimate of the Indochina Situation," 11 Sep 1950, RG 319, G-3, 091, Indochina TS; JCS memo for Secretary of Defense, JCS 1992/29, 7 Sep 1950, RG 218, CCS 092, Asia (6-25-48), section 6; "Substance of Statements Made at the Wake Island Conference," *FRUS*, 1950, 7: 948; Generals James Gavin and Paul Adams to CSUSA, "U.S. Policy Toward Indochina," 10 Aug 1954, RG 319, G-3, 091, Indochina; Army P&O Staff Study, "Long-Range (Thru FY 56) Program for Development of Minimum Forces Necessary to Provide Internal Security for South Vietnam," 2 Nov 1954, RG 319, G-3, Indochina.

7   Report by JIC to JCS on "Effect of a Cease-Fire in Korea on Chi Com Capabilities in Southeast Asia," JIC 529/6, 16 Aug 1951, RG 218, CCS 092, Asia (6-25-48), Section 16; JCS memo for Secretary of Defense, "U.S. Objectives and Courses of Action with Respect to Communist Aggression in Southeast Asia," *Ibid.*, Section 25; JCS memo for Secretary of Defense, "Department of State Draft Paper on Indochina," 18 Apr 1952, *Ibid.*, Section 28. Radford in U.S. Congress, Senate, Committee on Foreign Relations, *Executive Sessions of the Senate Foreign Relations Committee (Historical Series)*, Vol. VI, 83d Cong., 2d Sess., 1954: 116, 140, 211-218.

8   Intelligence Division Research Project, "Evaluation of the Situation in Indochina," 16 Mar 1950, RG 319, Bulky Package, OPS 091, Indochina TS; Army Map Service, "Terrain Estimate of Indochina," 6 Nov 1950, RG 319, 091, Indochina.

9   Cabell in memo by Assistant Secretary of State for Fear East Affairs (John Allison) to Secretary of State, 28 Jan 1953, *FRUS*, 1952-1954, 13(1): 366-369; The Intelligence division Map Service's, and Cabell's recognition of the difficulties involved in guerrilla war contrasts with Ronald Spector, *Advice and Support: The*

Early Years of the U.S. Army in Vietnam, 1941-1960 (New York) 1983: 168-169, who asserts that the American military underestimated the strength and ability of Viet Minh forces and consistently urged greater use of French firepower.

General Thomas Trapnell comments at debriefing, 3 May 1954, *US-VN Relations*, Book 9: 406-20; Chair of the JCS Radford, testifying at executive sessions of the SCFR in February 1954—the same time at which he was clamoring for U.S. combat support of French forces at Dien Bien Phu—conceded that the Viet Minh, without the need to hold territory, could determine the time, place and nature of military engagements. Without heavy equipment, Giap's forces could fade into mountains, forests or jungles and then regroup to attack elsewhere. The Viet Minh, moreover, could conduct operations with fewer guerrillas than France or the U.S. could with conventional troops. *Executive Sessions of the SCFR*, 6:116, 140, 211-8.

[10] Davis in *P.P.-Gravel*, I: 88-90.

[11] Ridgway memo to JCS, 6 Apr 1954, *FRUS*, 1952-54, 13 (1): 1269-70; Shepard memo for JCS, 2 Apr 1954, RG 218, Chair's File, Radford, CCS 091, Indochina (Apr 1954); Gavin, G-3, memo for CSUSA, "Military Implications of Cease-Fire Agreements in Indochina," 22 Jul 1954, RG 319, G-3, 091, Indochina; see Gavin memo, 17 Jul 1954, *Ibid.*

[12] After the Geneva Conference the JCS, again with Ridgway its most forceful member, opposed establishing a training mission to Indochina. Se, e.g., F.W. Moorman memo for Gavin, 11 May 1954, RG 319, CS, 091, and *US-VN Relations*, Book 1, III.A.2.: A-19, A-20; JCS memo for Secretary of Defense, 19 Oct 1954, "Development and Training of Indigenous Forces in Indochina," *US-VN Relations*, Book 10: 773-4; Gavin, *War and Peace in the Space Age* (New York) 1958; Ridgway, *Soldier*: 278.

[13] Douglas Kinnard, *The War Managers* (Hanover, NH) 1977: 81.

[14] General Maxwell Taylor, "The Current Situation in SVN—Nov. '64," *Declassified Documents Reference System* (Carrollton Press), (83), 000557 (hereafter cited as *DDRS* with appropriate year and document number); Taylor to Department of State, 21 Dec 1964, *DDRS* (79), 206D; M. Bundy to Johnson, Report of Taylor Backgrounder to Media, 24 Dec 1964, *DDRS* (79), 222C.

Taylor added that the signs of progress in south Viet Nam were often mixed. In November 1964 tension along the RVN-Cambodian border had risen and the anti-VC campaign in the south was not going well, but an RVN treasury bond progress got off to a good start with 700 million piasters (over $9 million) subscribed, primarily by financial institutions. "This is another example," Taylor observed, "of the odd contradictions which one often finds in the indicators of progress in this country. Almost never do they point in the same direction at the same time." Taylor to Department of State, 4 Nov 1964, *DDRS* (85), 001777.

[15] Westmoreland to Taylor, 24 Nov 1964, *DDRS* (77), 288E; ACS, J-3, MACV, to Westmoreland, Dec 1964 or Jan 1965, *DDRS* (78), 236C.

Aware of the RVN's difficulties and of the long task involved in American support of the government, General Taylor suggested that the U.S. might be willing to accommodate its policy toward Ho "If the DRV remain aloof from the CHI COMS in a Tito-like state," Taylor envisioned, "we would not be averse to aiding such a government provided it conducted itself decently with its neighbors." Taylor briefing, 27 Nov 1964, *P.P.-Gravel,* 3: 666-72, Document 242.

16 Taylor memo, 2 Feb 1965, *DDRS* (77), 34D; Westmoreland analysis, 25 Feb 1965, *P.P.-Gravel,* 3: 337-8.

17 Westmoreland in Embassy to Department of Defense, 5 Jun 1965, *DDRS* (79), 325A; JCS memo for Secretary of Defense, 27 Aug 1965, *Ibid.,* 381A.

18 Notes of Meeting on Vietnam, 22 Jul 1965, Papers of Lyndon B. Johnson, Meeting Notes File, Box 1, Folder: July 21-27 1965; Keith McCutcheon, Notes on Commanders' Conference, 14 Nov 1965, McCutcheon papers, Personal Collection 464, Box 14, Marine Corps Historical Center (hereafter cited as MCHC with P.C. and box numbers).

19 Taylor, Memorandum for the President, 12 Apr 1966, subject: Current Situation in South Viet-Nam, Lyndon B. Johnson Library, National Security File, Memos to the President, Walt Whitman Rostow, volume 1, box 1.

20 McCutcheon to Harry Pack, 12 Apr 1966, *Ibid.,* Box 15; Krulak to Admiral Sharp, 31 Mar 1966, to Baldwin, 19 Apr 1966, Krulak papers, PC 486, Box 1, MCHC.

Krulak added in a memo to Secretary of Defense McNamara on 9 May 1966 that the U.S. would "suffer a grave set back, unless it could get "a halter on Ky" and press Vietnamese political and military leaders to end their factional conflicts. *Ibid.*

21 *P.P-Gravel,* 2: 379.501.

22 Lansdale to Walt Rostow, 8 Nov 1966, subject: The Battleground in 1967, Lyndon B. Johnson Library, National Security File, Memos to the President, Walt Whitman Rostow, volume 15, box 11.

23 Taylor and Felt in *Ibid.,* 2: 83-92; Shoup in U.S. Congress, Senate, Committee on Foreign Relations, *Legislative Proposals Relating to the War in Southeast Asia,* 92d Cong., 1st Sess., 1971: 495; Westmoreland background briefing in Taylor to Department of State, 4 Sep 1964, *DDRS* (84), 000737.

Taylor agreed that the U.S. should not employ combat troops in Viet Nam and in November warned the Department of State that "too much" American presence could be as dangerous as too little and advised against sending American engineers and logistics units to the central provinces because they would constitute a combat force and incur casualties. Taylor to Department of State, 3 Nov 1964, *P.P.-Gravel,* 3: 590-1, Document 217; *Ibid.,* 14 Nov 1964, *DDRS* (83), 000553.

24 MACV Study in Taylor to Department of State, 6 Jan 1965, *DDRS* (83), 002793.

25 *P.P.-Gravel,* 3: 6, 448, 455; JCS memo for Secretary of Defense, 6 Apr 1965, *DDRS* (81), 70A.

26 Notes of Meeting on Vietnam, 22 Jul 1965, Lyndon B. Johnson Library, Meeting Notes File, box 1, folder: July 21-27 1965.

27 Wheeler, CJCS, to Secretary of Defense, 11 Jun 1965, *DDRS* (79), 270A; *Ibid.*, 27 Aug 1965, *DDRS* (79), 381A.

On President Johnson's July 1965 decision—which Larry Berman asserts meant that the U.S. decided "to lose the war slowly"—see *Planning a Tragedy: The Americanization of the War in Vietnam* (New York) 1982.

28 Dave Richard Palmer, *Summons of the Trumpet: U.S.-Vietnam in Perspective* (San Rafael, CA: Presidio) 1978: 110; Harry Summers, *On Strategy: A Critical Analysis of the Vietnam War* (Novato, CA: Presidio) 1982: 148; Taylor to Department of State, 3 Nov 1964, *P.P.-Gravel*, 3: 590-1, Document 217; Johnson in *U.S. News and World Report*, 7 Feb 1966: 28-29.

29 Palmer, *Ibid.*; Johnson, *Ibid.*

30 Lansdale, "Still the Search for Goals," *Foreign Affairs*, Oct 1968: 93; Dave Richard Palmer, *Readings in Current Military History* (West Point) 1969: 94.

31 On Westmoreland's optimism see *New York Times*, 20 Nov 1967: 1; White House report of Johnson's trip to Guam, 1967, *DDRS* (85), 002248; Kinnard, *War Managers:* 45, 74-5.

32 Hubert Humphrey in summary notes of the 578th Meeting of the National Security Council, 8 Nov 1967, *DDRS* (85), 001918; On Tet as a conclusive victory for the military see Westmoreland, *A Soldier Reports* (Garden City, NY) 1976: 436-7; Palmer, *Summons:* 252-5; General Winant Sidle, "The Tet Offensive: Another Press Controversy," in Harrison Salisbury, ed., *Vietnam Reconsidered: Lessons from a War* (New York) 1984: 164-6; Taylor, *Swords and Plowshares* (New York) 1972: 383.

On 1968 evaluations of Tet, see Westmoreland to Sharp, 12 Feb 1968, *DDRS* (79), 369A; Wheeler Report to Johnson, 27 Feb 1968, *DDRS* (79), 382B, 383A, *P.P.-Gravel*, 4: 546-9.

33 Johnson WDC 3166 to Westmoreland and Abrams, 1 Mar 1968, Record Group 319, Papers of William Childs Westmoreland, folder 380: Eyes Only Message File.

34 McGarr to Kennedy, 22 Feb 1962, *DDRS* (76), 33H.

35 Yarborough to Westmoreland, 26 Feb 1964, Westmoreland Papers, folder 460 [2 of 2], #3 History File, 20 Dec 1965 to 29 Jan 1966.

36 In October 1964 Taylor reported that pacification progress was "minimal at best" while a month later the CI program had "bogged down and will require heroic treatment to assure revival." Taylor to Department of State, 7 Oct 9164, *DDRS* (85), 001750; Taylor, "The Current Situation in SVN-November 1946," *Ibid.* (83), 000557; Westmoreland to Taylor, 24 Nov 1964, *Ibid.* (77), 288E; Westmoreland in *P.P.-Gravel*, 3: 337-8.

37 Taylor added that MACV's use of heavy weapons, particularly 155" and 8" howitzers, would "encourage the critics of U.S. policy who are saying that we are more concerned about fighting Red China than Viet Cong." Taylor to Department of State, 14 Apr 1965, *DDRS* (79), 211C; "A Strategic Concept for the RVN," June 1965, Krulak papers, PC 486, Box 1, MCHC.

38 *P.P.-Gravel*, 2: 576-80; Krulak to Greene, 7 Oct 1966, Krulak papers, PC 486, Box 2, MCHC.

39 U.S. Congress, Senate, Armed Services Committee, *Supplemental Military Procurement and Construction Authorizations, Fiscal Year 1966*, 89th Cong., 2d Sess., 1966: 274-8; Cf. *U.S. News and World Report*, 28 Feb 1966: 14.

Likewise, Krulak noted that if, somehow, all North Vietnamese soldiers in the south, and VC Main Force units in the RVN, were to "vaporize" the U.S. "would still have a tremendous war on our hands in Vietnam." Krulak to Cushman, 25 May 1967, Krulak papers, PC 486, Box 1, MCHC.

40 Wheeler CJCS 7859-66 to Westmoreland and Sharp, 21 Dec 1966, Westmoreland Papers, folder 362 (2): Eyes Only Message File.

41 Krulak to Don Neff, 25 Oct 1967, *Ibid.*, box 2; Krulak memo, March 1968, *Ibid.*; Anderson to McCutcheon, 19 Feb 1968, McCutcheon papers, PC 464, box 20, MCHC.

The Marines and Air Force were also involved in a dispute over operational control of certain facets of the air war. "In addition to fighting the VC," I Marine Aviation Wing (I MAW) Commander General Keith McCutcheon charged in early 1966, "we are still fighting the Air Force. They are like Notre Dame, they never give up. We are not going to give up either." Two years later the battle still raged. "Some of our biggest battles are with the other services, rather than the VC and NVA," General Anderson lamented. Such infighting took time better spent in battle against the enemy, Anderson explained, but people like Seventh Air Force General William Momyer refused to "give in one iota of the Air Force's party line." Likewise General G.S. Bowman found Air Force requests for resources to be "insatiable" and believed that "it has never occurred to them [Air Force officers] that the same type of priority and planning is required in the use of Air assets as is employed in the use of Ground assets." McCutcheon to Col. M.R. Yunck, 7 Feb 1966, 19 Feb 1968, *Ibid.*, box 20; Bowman to McCutcheon, 23 Dec 1969, *Ibid.*, box 23.

42 Bruce Palmer, *The 25-Year War: America's Military Role in Vietnam* (New York) 1985: 46, see also 213, n. 46; Kinnard, *War Managers*: 154.

43 David Shoup with James Donovan, "The New American Militarism," *The Atlantic Monthly*, Apr 1969: 51-56; Lansdale, "Still the Search for Goals": 94.

44 Larry Berman, *Planning a Tragedy: The Americanization of the War in Vietnam* (New York) 1982.

45 On the politics of military policy, see Mark Perry, *Four Stars* (Boston) 1989.

46 General Westmoreland's History Notes, entry for 9 Dec 1965, Westmoreland papers, folder 459: #2 History File, 25 October-20 December 1965; Msg, Westmoreland MAC 1658 to Sharp and Wheeler, 17 February 1967, Westmoreland papers, folder 363: Eyes Only Message File.

47 Msg, Wheeler CJCS 1810-67 to Westmoreland, 9 Mar 1967, Westmoreland v. CBS, DA/WNRC Files, Box 2, folder: Suspense; for figures see Msg, Wheeler JCS 1843-67 to Westmoreland, 11 Mar 1967, Westmoreland papers, folder 364:

COMUSMACV Message File; Jim Jones, Memorandum to the President, 12 Sep 1967, subject: Weekly Luncheon, Lyndon B. Johnson Library, Meeting Notes File, Box 2, folder: Sep 12, 1967.

[48] Indeed, the spector of Viet Nam was prominent during the recent Gulf War. As he addressed a national television audience at the start of the war, George Bush claimed that "our troops... will not be asked to fight with one hand tied behind their back." After the war had ended, Bush boasted that "by God, we've kicked the 'Vietnam syndrome' once and for all." *Washington Post,* 17 Jan and 2 Mar 1991.

[49] See, for instance, Clark Clifford with Richard Holbrooke, "Annals of Government (The Vietnam Years-Part II), *New Yorker* (13 May 1991); I have more fully developed the argument that the military understood that Tet had indeed been an American failure in "The Myth of Tet: Military Failure and the Politics of War," a chapter in my doctoral dissertation which I would be pleased to share with interested readers.

[50] On public reaction to Tet and the reinforcement request, see Peter Braestrup, *Big Story* (New Haven) 1983, and Kathleen Turner, *Lyndon Johnson's Dual War: Vietnam and the Press* (Chicago) 1985.

[51] Msg, Wheeler JCS 1589 to Westmoreland, 9 Feb 1968, Westmoreland v. CBS, Litigation Collection, Box 20, folder: MACV Backchannel Messages to Westmoreland, 1-28 February 1968; Msg, Johnson WDC 2515 to Palmer, 17 Feb 1968, *Ibid.*

[52] Record of COMUSMACV Fonecon with General Palmer, 0850, 25 Feb 1968, subject: Discussion, Westmoreland papers, folder 1450: Fonecons, February 1968; Neil Sheehan, *A Bright Shining Lie: John Paul Vann and America in Vietnam* (New York) 1988: 720.

[53] Westmoreland paper, "The Origins of the Post-Tet 1968 Plans for Additional Forces in the Republic of Vietnam," Apr 1970, Westmoreland papers, folder 493 [1 of 2]: #37 History Files, 1 January-30 June 1970; Westmoreland, *A Soldier Reports* (Garden City, NY) 1976: 469.

[54] On the political uses of Viet Nam see, among others, Walter LaFeber, "The Last War, the Next War, and the New Revisionists," and Marilyn B. Young, "This Is Not a Pipe," *Middle East Report* (Jul-Aug 1991): 21.24.

[55] For a detailed consideration of Shoup's, Ridgway's, and Gavin's public criticism of the war see Buzzanco, "The American Military's Rationale Against the Vietnam War."

[56] Shoup speech of 14 May 1966 in SCFR, Present Situation in Vietnam (1968): 47; Matthew Ridgway, The Korean War (Garden City: New York) 1967: 250; Ridgway in New York Times, 14 Mar 1970: 30; Ridgway to McGovern, 18 Oct 1972, Matthew Ridgway Papers, Military History Institute, Carlisle Barracks, PA, Box 34A (hereafter cited as Ridgway Papers, MHI, with appropriate box number); Gavin in U.S. Congress, Senate, Committee on Foreign Relations, *Moral and Military Aspects of the War In Southeast Asia,* 91st Cong., 2d Sess., 1970: 79.

Marine Colonel William Corson, in his well-received 1968 book *The Betrayal*, likewise scorned President Johnson's "conventional wisdom" on America's mission in Viet Nam, which accounted for "only one explanation of the facts and but one way to achieve salvation." That approach, Corson charged, was "specious, dangerous, nonsense." *The Betrayal* (New York) 1968: 9.

[57] Transcript of Gavin Interview on "Meet the Press," 12 Nov 1967; Transcript of Shoup Interview with Rep. William Ryan, 19 Dec 1967, in David Shoup biographical file, Marine Corps Historical Center (hereafter cited as Shoup file, MCHC); Shoup in SCFR, *Present Situation in Vietnam* (1968): 3, 14.

[58] Gavin in *Newsweek*, 16 Oct 1967: 28-9; Gavin, *Crisis Now* (New York) 1968: 66; Gavin in U.S. Congress, Senate, Committee on Foreign Relations, *Conflicts Between United States Capabilities and Foreign Commitments*, 90th Cong., 1st Sess., 1967: 7.

[59] Gavin in U.S. Congress, Senate, Committee on Foreign Relations, *Supplemental Foreign Assistance Act, Fiscal Year 1966—Vietnam*, 89th Cong., 2d Sess., 1966: 228-31, 235, 258-60 (these hearings were televised nationally and later edited and released as *The Vietnam Hearings* and will be hereafter cited as that); Ridgway to James Wilson, 17 Nov 1966, Ridgway Papers, MHI, Box 34A.

[60] Transcript of Gavin Interview on "Meet the Press," 12 Nov 1967; Shoup in SCFR, *Present Situation in Vietnam* (1968): 15-7; James Donovan, *Militarism U.S.A.* (New York) 1970: 157.

[61] Shoup in SCFR, *Present Situation in Vietnam* (1968): 15-7; Transcript of Gavin Interview on "Meet the Press," 12 Nov 1967; Gavin in SCFR, *Moral and Military Aspects* (1970): 60-1.

[62] James Gavin, "A Communication on Vietnam," *Harper's Magazine* (Feb 1966): 16-20; in SCFR, *Vietnam Hearings* (1966): 228-35.

The Air Force and Marines had in fact advocated enclave strategies at the outset of the U.S. troop commitment to Viet Nam but were challenged and overruled by Westmoreland, Wheeler, and Army Chief Johnson—all advocates of active if not unlimited combat involvement by American forces. *P.P.-Gravel*, 3: 397.

[63] For positive appraisals of Gavin's enclaves strategy see *Harper's*, (Mar 1966): 6, and (Apr): 6; *Newsweek* (3 Jan 1966); *Christian Science Monitor* (27 Jan 1966): 1; *National Review* (22 Feb 1966): 151.

For criticism of Gavin see *Christian Science Monitor* (31 Jan 1966): 1; George Ball in White House memo, 2 Nov 1967, *DDRS* (85), 002225; on Westmoreland see *P.P.-Gravel*, 3: 394-5, 479; on Taylor see *Ibid.* and *New York Times*, 4 Feb 1966: 1.

[64] Shoup speech of 14 May 1966, in SCFR, *Present Situation in Vietnam* (1968): 44-51; Ridgway, "Pull-Out, All-Out, or Stand Fast in Vietnam?" *Look* (5 Apr 1966): 84.

[65] Hester in *Miami Herald* (20 Jan 1967) in Shoup file, MCHC, and in *New York Times* (23 Sep 1969): 46; Ridgway, *Korean War:* 250; Bouker press release in Shoup file, MCHC; Shoup in SCFR, *Legislative Proposals* (1971): 487.

66   On public impact of Generals' critique see Buzzanco, "The American Military's Rationale Against the Vietnam War": 574-6; Gavin in *Newsweek* (16 Oct 1967): 29; Gavin in SCFR, *Moral and Military Aspects* (1970): 65; Spock in Charles DeBennedetti, *The Peace Reform in American History* (Bloomington) 1980: 176.

67   Gavin in SCFR, *Moral and Military Aspects* (1970): 84-5; Transcript of Shoup interview with John Scali on ABC-Scope, Shoup file, MCHC. Collins, Interview at Combat Studies Institute, Army Command and General Staff College: 14, MHI.

68   Lansdale in Ridgway's "Comments on the Asprey Paper," 1 Dec 1972, Ridgway Papers, MHI, Box 34B.

69   Westmoreland Oral History (1), 8 Feb 1969, Lyndon B. Johnson Library, 12-3.

70   Ridgeway Interview/Question Period at Command General Staff College, 1984: 22-3, Ridgway Papers, MHI.

United States Policy Towards Vietnam, 1954-1955: The Stabilization of the Diem Government

Asad Ismi

American military involvement in Vietnam and its failure were brought on by the absence of an effective government in South Vietnam. As R.W. Komer, director of the pacification program during 1968-69, put it:

> In retrospect perhaps the greatest single restraint on the US' ability to achieve its aims in Vietnam was the sheer incapacity of the regimes we backed... The lack of a sufficiently viable, functioning government was a crucial handicap.[1]

This handicap can be traced back to the Eisenhower Administration's decision in May 1955 to support the government of Ngo Dinh Diem in its effort to turn South Vietnam into an anti-Communist bulwark. In spite of arguments to the contrary by General J. Lawton Collins (US Representative in South Vietnam) the Administration elected to pursue a negative policy, forsaking the aim of building a viable state in favor of denying South Vietnam to the Communists and the French. This critical decision tied US prestige to a repressive dictatorship and an unstable state, the impending collapse of which drew the US into war in 1965. The significance of the Collins Mission (sent to South Vietnam from November 1954 to May 1955) lay in the fact that it revealed Diem's incapacity to form a viable government from the outset and gave the US the opportunity to look for alternatives or, failing that, to withdraw from Vietnam. In April 1955 when Diem faced armed internal opposition, the US almost took this chance but by then the covert arm of its policy had become too involved in sustaining Diem in power. The CIA's success in saving Diem's position was in turn used by Secretary of State John Foster Dulles to justify unconditional US support for the Prime Minister. Collins may have won the argument too late but his objections to Diem remained valid and set the stage for American failure in Vietnam.

Following the end of the Geneva Conference on 22 July 1954, the US set out to build South Vietnam into an anti-Communist bastion by supporting Diem who had been appointed Prime Minister by Emperor Bao Dai on 19 June and took office on 7 July. US post-Geneva policy towards Vietnam was aimed at achieving three objectives: denying South Vietnam to the Communists, removing French influence from there, and setting up a viable government and nation-state under Diem. The latter was certainly anti-Communist and anti-French enough to fulfill the first two objectives, but could he set up a viable government? Military and intelligence estimates were pessimistic about this possibility and in November the greatest challenge to the policy of supporting Diem was launched by General J. Lawton Collins, who was sent by Eisenhower to stabilize the Diem government.

As expressed in NSC5429 the main tenets of the new policy involved negotiating a Collective Defense Treaty for Southeast Asia, direct aid to the Diem Government and military training for the Vietnamese National Armed Forces (VNAF).   From the outset this policy faced tremendous obstacles. Chaos prevailed in South Vietnam where internal opposition paralyzed the Diem Government; the French argued for Diem's removal and the Pentagon opposed giving direct aid or assigning a training mission. By the end of October, Dulles had overridden French and military opposition but the situation inside South Vietnam remained unstable even as the US rapidly moved towards becoming the guarantor of its existence.

Publicly, the Administration tried to put the best face possible on the Geneva settlement but privately it saw the agreement as a major setback for US policy in Southeast Asia. NSC5429/2, approved on 20 August, concluded that Geneva was a "disaster" that "completed a major forward stride of Communism which may lead to the loss of Southeast Asia." The US had to prevent further Communist advances by negotiating a Southeast Asia Security Treaty and giving economic and military aid to Laos, Cambodia and South Vietnam.[2] The first phase of NSC 5429 was completed with the signing of the Southeast Asia Collective Defense Treaty, which became known as SEATO (Southeast Asia Treaty Organization) by the US, Britain, France, Australia, New Zealand, the Philippines, Thailand and Pakistan on 8 September in Manila. To avoid explicitly violating Geneva a protocol was added to the treaty extending SEATO protection to Cambodia, Laos and South Vietnam without making them actual members.[3]

The second phase of NSC5429/2 involved support for the Diem government and South Vietnam. The US' decision to support Diem, as it evolved during 1954-1955, has been termed "the most fundamental" of its thirty-year involvement in Vietnam.[4] It signified a major policy shift away from working through the French and towards assuming primary responsibility for maintaining a non-Communist Vietnam. The direct linking of US prestige to the survival of South Vietnam in turn set the stage for American military intervention in 1965. Dulles blamed the French for the loss of North Vietnam and wanted them "completely out of the rest of Indochina" so the US could work directly with the "native leadership" to "salvage what the Communists had ostensibly left out of their grasp."

On 17 August 1954 the Secretary discussed giving direct US aid to the Associated States with Eisenhower, and the President agreed to do so (this was announced on 29 September).[5] The next day Dulles wrote to French Prime Minister Pierre Mendès-France that the Diem government provided "a nucleus for future efforts." To "dissipate the present discouragement in Vietnam" and remove the impression that it was abandoning Indochina, the US was now ready to give direct aid to the Associated States, and to consider their requests for direct military training.[6] Dulles was referring to the chaotic situation in South Vietnam where Diem controlled hardly a "few blocks of Saigon." The gangster Binh Xuyen sect (involved in gambling, prostitution and narcotics) which ran the National Police, controlled the rest,[7] while the Vietminh dominated the countryside along with the Cao Dai and Hoa Hao politico-religious sects. The Vietnamese National Army (VNA) had broken down completely with many battalions being depleted by desertions to the Vietminh[8] and its French-appointed Chief of Staff, General Nguyen Van Hinh, was soon maneuvering to overthrow Diem. The sects also opposed Diem,[9] and the US suspected the French of giving "quiet encouragement" to Hinh,[10] and "actively undermining Diem."[11] According to a National Intelligence Estimate dated 3 August, the chances of establishing a strong regime in South Vietnam were poor and the situation was likely to "continue to deteriorate progressively over the next year...." The Geneva Agreements had "engendered an atmosphere of frustration and disillusionment [in South Vietnam] ... compounded by widespread uncertainty as to French and US intentions."[12]

While instability in Saigon stimulated Dulles to increase American support for Diem, it generated significant resistance to this policy from the French and the Department of Defense. French Minister for the Associated States, Guy La Chambre, considered Diem "totally ineffective in reconciling the anti-Communist elements in... Vietnam and producing a government which commands wide popular support,"[13] and the JCS opposed assigning a training mission to MAAG Saigon in the absence of a "strong, stable, civil government in control."[14] In a series of talks in Washington from 27 to 29 September, Walter Bedell Smith (Under Secretary of State) was able to persuade La Chambre that France and the US had to "bolster Diem without reservations and give him a chance to succeed."[15] Dulles overrode the military's opposition by reversing the JCS' argument: the Secretary insisted that training the VNA was "one of the most efficient means" of strengthening the Vietnamese government."[16]

The instability in Saigon however persisted. From August to November 1954 Diem appeared to be on the verge of being overthrown by General Hinh and only the support of US Ambassador Donald Heath saved the Prime Minister from six coup attempts.[17] To sort out this "confused situation" which had reached a "critical stage" Dulles expressed the need for a high-ranking US official (preferably an Army officer) to be sent to South Vietnam. Eisenhower did not hesitate to recommend General J. Lawton Collins.[18]

"Lighting Joe" had been one of Eisenhower's most successful Corps Commanders during WWII and as Army Chief of Staff Eisenhower had picked him to be his deputy. During the Korean War, Collins had served as Army Chief of Staff. Eisenhower had great trust in Collins' judgement and ability and this was reflected in the terms of the General's appointment.[19] The President designated Collins Special US Representative with the personal rank of Ambassador, and gave him "broad authority to direct, utilize and control all agencies and resources of the US government in Vietnam." The main task of the Collins Mission was to "coordinate and direct a program in support of the Diem Government to enable it to... establish... control throughout [South Vietnam]... promote internal security and political and economic stability and counteract Vietminh influence..."[20]

Collins' first priority after his arrival in Saigon on 8 November was to remove General Hinh who posed the most urgent threat to the Diem government. On 11 November Collins made clear to Hinh that "if he revolted... he would have to stand alone... US aid would definitely be withdrawn."[21] Hinh left for France on 18 November. Collins next concentrated on taking over the VNA's training from the French and broadening the Diem government. Collins' negotiations with French Commissioner General Paul Ely on training the VNA proceeded rapidly and by 13 December the two had signed an agreement. The "Understanding on Development and Training of an Autonomous Vietnamese Armed Forces (VNAF)" stated that 1) the VNAF would be reduced from 170,000 to 85,000 (organized into six divisions) by 1 July 1955, 2) France would grant full autonomy to the VNAF by 1 July 1955, 3) Chief US MAAG (Military Assistance Advisory Group) would take over the training and organization of the VNAF on 1 January 1955 under the overall authority of General Ely, and 4) all US and French trainers and advisers would be under the authority of MAAG; as the VNAF's "efficiency" increased, the number of US and French trainers would be decreased.[22]

Collins was however unable to persuade Diem to broaden his government, which made the General conclude that there was nothing viable in South Vietnam to stabilize. Diem, Collins saw, was not interested in setting up an effective government—one which could delegate power and implement reforms—but in monopolizing power in his family. Given this, Collins urged Diem's removal and viewed US withdrawal from Vietnam as the only sensible course of action. Dulles however stood solidly behind Diem and this prolonged debate was to determine the future of US policy in Vietnam. Collins' doubts about Diem had diminished by the end of January 1955 only to flare up in March.

Collins' rapid disillusionment with Diem stemmed from the latter's refusal to appoint Phan Huy Quat Defense Minister. A leader of the northern Dai Viet Party, Quat had served in previous cabinets[23] and was considered by Collins to be a "first-rate man" for the post of Defense

Minister. Collins felt a strong individual was needed in this post to ensure the VNA's loyalty and render it capable of establishing internal security, both prerequisites to stabilizing the Diem government.[24] Collins saw in Diem's refusal to appoint Quat an attempt to create a family dictatorship. The Ambassador perceived as one of Diem's major faults his inability to delegate authority outside the immediate Ngo family circle.[25] It was obvious to Collins that Diem's family was the real power behind him; Ngo Dinh Nhu, Diem's brother, was his closest political adviser, while Nhu's wife acted as his official hostess. Brothers Can, Thuc and Luyen controlled Annam, gathered Catholic support and acted as Ambassador to Britain respectively, and a close relative, Tran Van Do, was Foreign Minister.[26] According to Collins, Nhu and his wife exerted such a powerful influence on Diem that no one outside the family with any ability was going to have any "real part" in the government. Diem and Nhu feared Quat's ability and so were afraid to let him or any other strong man control the army. They also saw Quat as a potential successor to Diem. Collins realized that now that he had removed Hinh and given Diem effective control of the VNA, it was unlikely that Diem would delegate real authority to anyone, preferring to "maintain [a] meddling hand" to the detriment of the training mission and "effective development" of the VNAF.[27] Given this situation, Collins cabled Dulles on 16 December that the only viable course of action was withdrawal from Vietnam unless Bao Dai could be brought back. Diem, Collins stated, was incapable of decisive leadership without which South Vietnam could not be saved.[28]

Dulles, however, let the Ambassador know on 24 December, first that there was no alternative to Diem, second that "even a slight chance of success in Vietnam was worth considerable investment... If only to buy time [to] build up strength elsewhere in [the] area[29] and third that replacing Diem would mean "... the selection of a successor which would appear dictated by the French."[30] Dulles had no illusions about Diem's competence. On 19 December he admitted to Mendès-France that Diem seemed "constitutionally incapable of making decisions."[31] But the Secretary knew that (as Former Ambassador to Saigon, Donald Heath put it) there was no one to take Diem's place "who would serve US objectives any better."[32] There was no one more anti-French and anti-Communist than Diem.

Dulles' arguments failed to sway Collins but, luckily for the Secretary, the situation inside South Vietnam took a turn for the better at the beginning of 1955. The success of a trip Collins had encouraged Diem to take through South Annam tempered the Ambassador's previously gloomy assessment and on 5 January Collins wrote to Dulles that the Prime Minister was gaining popularity and was now putting emphasis on decision-making.[33] Thus it was a relatively optimistic Status Report on Vietnam that Collins submitted to the NSC on 20 January, which concluded that in an overall sense Diem was "the best available Prime Minister to lead Vietnam."[34]

In its first three months the Collins Mission was able to accomplish a great deal. Significant steps were taken towards the stabilization of the Diem government with the removal of Hinh and the taking over of military training from the French. However, the Collins-Dulles debate over the replacement of Diem revealed that the objectives of US policy in Vietnam had become contradictory. With Diem it was possible to deny South Vietnam to the Communists and the French, but not to build a viable nation-state or government. The question was which of the objectives was more important. The negative ones or the positive one? Was the aim of building a viable state secondary to its anti-Communist, anti-French nature? For Collins the answer was clearly "No," but for Dulles it seemed to be "Yes." Collins had come to Vietnam to build an effective government. He had removed Hinh and undertaken the VNA's training for this purpose and not to set up a dictatorship. When he thought this was happening he had argued for a positive policy: replacing Diem with someone around whom a government could be built.

For Dulles, on the other hand, the quality of South Vietnamese leadership was a secondary matter. As the Secretary told Mendès-France on 19 December:

> Only serious problem we have not yet solved is that of indigenous leadership. We cannot expect it to be solved ideally because there is no tradition among indigenous people for self-government. We must get along with something less good than best.[35]

As long as Diem served the US' negative objectives he had to be supported. The US had to give him control of the Army, remove his Vietnamese challengers and curb French influence. With the Army, Diem could deal with any further internal threats to his position.

Hence, for Dulles, South Vietnam could not be saved without Diem, and for Collins, it could not be saved with him. Dulles had won the first round of the debate but this was a temporary victory. The problem of Diem remained and was splitting the Administration's policy into two competing approaches. Events in March, 1955 led to the final contest between proponents of the negative and positive aspects of this policy.

Collins' optimism about Diem did not last long. During February Diem moved to take control of Saigon and the National Police away from the Binh Xuyen while simultaneously isolating the latter from the other sects by splitting the Cao Dai and Hoa Hao with bribes to selected leaders. Diem, however, carried out his anti-sect moves by by-passing his cabinet and with the help of his brothers Nhu and Luyen and CIA operative Colonel Edward G. Lansdale. This revived Collins' fears of a family dictatorship and renewed the Collins-Dulles debate on replacing Diem. This time, however, Collins was faced with significant opposition from the man sent by Dulles to keep Diem in power—Lansdale.

After French payments to the sects stopped on 1 February, Diem refused to renew the Binh Xuyen's gambling license which expired on 15 January.[36] Diem also rejected the other sects' demands that he integrate their troops into the VNA intact,[37] subsidize them, recognize their autonomy and reserve cabinet posts for them.[38] Instead, with funds secretly supplied by the CIA, Diem (through Lansdale) bought off key Cao Dai and Hoa Hao leaders and absorbed some of their troops into the VNA.[39] "In a succession of swift moves that left each sect leader wondering whether his sworn ally of yesterday had not sold him out for a substantial sum," Diem bought Cao Dai Generals Thé and Phuong for $2 million and $3.6 million respectively, and the Hoa Hao chief Soai for $3 million. Bernard Fall estimates that "the total amount of American dollars spent on bribes during March and April 1955 may well have gone beyond $12 million."[40]

Alarmed by Diem's maneuvering, the sects formed a "United Front of Nationalist Forces" on 1 March and issued an ultimatum to Diem on the 21st demanding that he replace his cabinet with one approved by the sects within five days.[41] This did not discourage Diem from seeking a confrontation with the Binh Xuyen, which he finally forced on the night of 29 March. At midnight about eighty Binh Xuyen troops stormed the Saigon-Cholon prefectural police headquarters which the sect had handed over to the VNA two days before on Bao Dai's instructions. As a result of increased tension between Diem and the sect leaders, the VNA had confined several Binh Xuyen troops in the headquarters. The Binh Xuyen attack was intended either to free those held or to reoccupy the building. The Binh Xuyen was able to do neither—by 1:30AM VNA forces had repulsed the attack,[42] and fighting ended by 3:30AM on 30 March, at which time a "French-imposed, US supported" cease fire went into effect.[43]

Collins' initial reaction was to support Diem and hold the Binh Xuyen responsible for the outbreak of violence.[44] Ely, on the other hand, was outraged at Diem's attitude and told Collins at 3PM on 30 March that Diem's use of force might lead to a long and bloody civil war.[45] The collapse of Diem's cabinet changed Collins' mind and brought his position closer to Ely's. At 6pm on 30 March Collins was informed that Foreign Minister Tran Van Do and the Ministers for Public Health and Social Action had resigned from the cabinet. Collins considered this "[a] most grave political crisis since without prompt formation of [a] new cabinet which will be most difficult Diem will essentially be governing alone." Do explained to Ely that he had resigned to make Diem resume negotiations with the sects and to force him to form a new government.[46] Though Collins was able to persuade Do and his colleagues to withdraw their resignations,[47] this incident convinced him that Diem would not be able to "change his nature"[48] and compelled him to call for the Prime Minister's removal. Consequently on 31 March Collins sent Dulles a "shocking analysis."[49] It stated that Generals Ty [VNA Chief of Staff] and

Nguyen Van Vy (Inspector General) showed no "enthusiasm" for engaging in a civil war or for Diem, who was now "almost entirely isolated" and "operating practically [a] one-man government with his two brothers Nhu and Luyen as principal advisors." Collins seriously doubted this could last long, as the country would not tolerate "government by family." Therefore, alternatives to Diem had to be considered. Collins suggested four men who he thought should replace Diem, with Tran Van Do as his preferred candidate. This presented the best chance of creating a broader government. If Do refused, the "next best choice" was Quat and, failing that, Bao Dai could return either to support a new government or to set up his own. Diem, Collins stated, had had a "fair chance to establish effective government" but had "produced little if anything of a constructive nature." The US had done everything in its power to "support and aid him" and to alter "his method of operating." Even the French under Ely had given Diem positive support. Collins concluded that Diem had shown himself unable to work "with anyone but his brothers" and had to bear most of the responsibility for the "critical situation" in which he now found himself.[50]

Dulles was taken aback by Collins' cable.[51] The Secretary replied on 1, 4 and 9 April that he thought they had agreed that the decision to support Diem had gone to "the point of no return." He did not doubt Collins' criticisms of Diem,[52] but stressed that US policy was "still pinned to the inescapable fact" that there was no alternative to Diem[53] who, Dulles continued to believe, could be persuaded to broaden his government with competent ministers.[54]   For the Secretary any alternative choice or combination offered far less of a chance of producing results than the present course.[55] Also Diem's replacement would mean giving in to French colonialism while "paying the bill" in Vietnam—any successor would know who held the real power, and US influence in Vietnam and elsewhere would be gravely weakened. A third concern was Congress, where Senator Mike Mansfield (Democrat/Montana) was "adamantly opposed" to abandoning Diem and could block US aid to Vietnam if the Administration did so.[56]

The problem, as Dulles saw it, was whether a central government with authority could develop in Vietnam. Diem had to be given "freedom of action" to meet the Binh Xuyen challenge "head on." In this context, the sect crisis revealed nothing new about Diem "but rather a basic and dangerous misunderstanding between France and the US." Both countries had agreed to support Diem despite his faults but, whereas the US had worked on the assumption that Diem would be supported against any challenger, the French wished to maintain the Binh Xuyen as an independent authority and would not let Diem deal with it.[57] Dulles opposed the truce as it put Diem and a gangster group on an equal basis and felt that the French had to be pressed strongly to support Diem in his assertion of authority over the Binh Xuyen. The VNA was strong and loyal enough to carry out this task given US and French backing.[58]

Dulles therefore did not think that replacing Diem was "desirable or practical at present"[59] and suggested an "intermediate solution" according to which Diem would be permitted to subdue the Binh Xuyen and thereby restore his "damaged prestige" while at the same time the government would be broadened with "other elements" who would be delegated real authority.[60]

Dulles' arguments failed to alter Collins' "firm conviction" that Diem did not have the capacity to unite his people and thereby save South Vietnam from Communism.[61] The Ambassador insisted that the US had to act as soon as possible, since the tenuous truce could explode at any time.[62] Faced with Collins' unyielding position Dulles asked him on 16 April to come to Washington to discuss Diem's replacement. An effective change-over, Dulles felt, could not be accomplished until Collins had consulted with the President, State and Defense Departments, CIA officials and, especially, with Congressional leaders.[63]

Having advised Diem to do everything possible to avoid conflict with the Binh Xuyen in his absence,[64] Collins arrived in Washington on 21 April. Over the next week the General met Eisenhower, Dulles, State and Defense Department and CIA representatives. By 27 April Collins had persuaded official Washington that Diem would have to be replaced. Collins reported to Eisenhower over lunch on 22 April that the Ngo family's monopoly of power had made the Diem government unsupportable. The Ambassador rejected the President's argument that the French were undermining Diem by stating that Eisenhower had received "inadequate and inaccurate intelligence," most of it emanating from the Palace. According to Collins, the only workable plan was one in which Quat would replace Diem under Bao Dai's aegis, which would in turn allow the Binh Xuyen to relinquish police powers.[65]

During two long meetings in the State Department the same day, Collins forcefully reiterated his view that Vietnam could not be saved as long as Diem remained in office. Diem could not delegate authority, focus on essential matters or initiate ideas and suggestions; he had no organized support or popularity and was governing alone with advice from his brothers. Collins warned that the present situation in Saigon was very tense and could "ignite" rapidly at any time, and concluded by saying that, although continued support for Diem was detrimental to US interest and a new arrangement was "urgently required," the State Department was reluctant to admit a failure in US policy and "obviously" would attempt to keep Diem in government in some position.[66]

Despite the opposition of his staff officers, Kenneth T. Young (Director of the Office of Philippine and South East Asian Affairs) and Robert D. Murphy (Deputy Under-Secretary of State for Political Affairs)[67] Dulles agreed with Collins on 27 April (as he stated in two telegrams sent to Paris and Saigon at 6:10 and 6:11PM) that "some change in political arrangements in Vietnam may be inevitable." Dulles was, however, determined to disguise American manipulation of the Vietnamese political process and retain Diem in some capacity if possible. The US would ostensibly maintain full support for Diem while the Vietnamese in Saigon apparently acted as the framers of a new government. Actually, Dulles admitted, Ely and Collins would be "the catalysts" of the change. They would inform Diem that due to his inability to create a broad-based coalition government and because of domestic resistance to him, their governments could no longer prevent his removal from power. Collins and Ely would urge Diem to serve in a new position but, if he refused, the change "would be carried out anyway" with every effort being made "to keep the Vietnamese label." Executive authority would be transferred to Quat or Do as President and Vice-President respectively.[68]

Dulles' two cables were never implemented. Before his plan could be put into operation, telegrams from Lansdale started arriving at 8PM on 27 April, detailing the outbreak of fighting in Saigon between the Binh Xuyen and the VNA. Lansdale stated that the Army's morale was high and argued that the US should continue supporting Diem.[69] Dulles responded by sending blocking cables to Paris and Saigon at 11:56PM which suspended all action on the previous telegrams.[70] The VNA's subsequent rout of the Binh Xuyen, combined with strong, vocal Congressional support for Diem, persuaded the Administration to restore full US support to Diem.

In saving Diem a crucial role was played by Lansdale. Collins' arguments had persuaded the bureaucrats in Washington that Diem had to be removed but he had never convinced the CIA operative of Diem's dispensability. After the 30 March ceasefire (which Lansdale had opposed), while Collins warned Diem against provoking violence and argued with Dulles for the Prime Minister to be replaced, Lansdale continued to strengthen Diem by dividing his opponents, and lent his support to the Prime Minister at key junctures, culminating in his 28 April cables (received on 27 April in Washington), which frustrated Collins' efforts to remove Diem. Lansdale's support was critical during April when Diem was virtually isolated. He no longer had a government, just a junta made up of the three Ngo brothers. VNA generals were unwilling to engage in civil war,[71] and the French, with whom Diem's relations had been rapidly deteriorating, had moved thousands of troops into Saigon to protect "French zones," which happened to include many fortified Binh Xuyen positions, while refusing Diem permission to bring three more battalions into the city.[72] Each day the Binh Xuyen expanded their hold on Saigon-Cholon by taking over more and more strategic positions.[73] Worst of all, while his enemies gained strength, Diem's friends seemed to be abandoning him. That a major review of US foreign policy was taking place was well known to Americans and French reporters,[74] and Collins' departure for Washington was followed by speculation in Saigon newspapers about the identity of Diem's possible successors. Minister of Reconstruction, Nguyen Van Thoai and Quat were mentioned as "American recommendations."[75]

Such reports signified the vacuum in policymaking left by Collins' absence, which was filled by Lansdale's determination to keep Diem in power. During February-March, Lansdale had secured for Diem the two most important assets in the forthcoming fight against the Binh Xuyen; Trin Minh Thé, who led three thousand of the Cao Dai's most seasoned fighters, and Colonel Duong Van Minh, who commanded eleven of the best French-trained VNA battalions[76], and to whom Lansdale had made available "ample discretionary funds."[77] Now Lansdale continually pressed the US Embassy to support Diem,[78] and arranged for Colonel Thai Hoang Minh, the Chief of Staff of the Binh Xuyen forces to "rally" to the Prime Minister with four battalions personally loyal to him.[79]

With Lansdale on his side, Diem, fully aware that the US might be conspiring to replace him, acted to safeguard his position. The Prime Minister issued a decree on 26 April replacing the Binh Xuyen Director General of the Police, Sang, with Colonel Nguyen Ngoc Le. Sang refused to obey, saying only Bao Dai could remove him[80] and the Binh Xuyen ignored this obvious provocation, secure in the belief that Bao Dai would remove Diem by 1 May, and that France and the US would withdraw support from him before then.[81]

The Binh Xuyen therefore had no reason to break the truce on 28 April, while Diem had little to lose and plenty to gain. By 11AM[82] a gun battle had begun around a Binh Xuyen position at 1115 Rue Petrushky in Cholon, resulting in twenty to thirty casualties.[83] Though it was not clear who fired the first shot, the VNA had been transported to Cholon in trucks,[84] while the Binh Xuyen appeared to be defending their area. At 12:15PM several mortar shells, fired by unknown persons, fell in a Binh Xuyen area near "Y" bridge, wounding six or seven French soldiers guarding an electric power plant.[85] At the same time, according to Lansdale's memoirs, Diem summoned him to the Palace and asked him intently whether it was true (as had been reported to Diem) that Collins had obtained Eisenhower's approval to "dump" Diem for a coalition government. Diem "relaxed a little" at Lansdale's reassurance that the US still supported him,[86] (which, according to Lansdale, was what Collins had told him before leaving for Washington).[87] In response to attacks on their positions, the Binh Xuyen fired mortars at the Presidential Palace at 1:15PM. When the shelling did not stop, Diem sent the VNA into action,[88] and the battle for Saigon was at last under way. Lansdale remained in close contact with Diem during the fighting.

Worried that Diem might have been correct about the change in US policy, Lansdale promptly informed Washington about the rapidly changing situation.[89] When queried by Allen Dulles (Director of the CIA) about Diem's prospects in the battle on the 28th,[90] Lansdale sent a "flood of reports and recommendations"[91] arguing that Diem was the best leader for Vietnam; his overthrow would mean a Vietminh victory and, even if ousted, Diem would remain in Vietnam as a potent anti-French opposition politician.[92] One such message was sent in the late afternoon from the US Embassy, where Lansdale had gone after observing the VNA performing well against the Binh Xuyen. Lansdale was astonished to see senior Embassy officials debating how to describe the VNA's low morale in the fighting and insisted on sending his own cable to Washington to counter such pessimistic estimates.[93]

Lansdale's enthusiasm for saving Diem was bound to lead him to encroach upon areas which feel within Collins' authority. On the same day the Colonel told Randolph Kidder, Chargé at the US Embassy and Collins' Deputy Chief of Mission, that the Saigon Country Team should express collective support for Diem; if that proved impossible, separate endorsements should be given by Agency heads. Kidder refused both requests, afraid that Lansdale was trying to usurp Collins' authority,[94] and Frank Meloy, Chief of the Embassy's political section, accused Lansdale of attempting to use the Country Team to oppose Collins.[95] An even sharper accusation against Lansdale was made by Armand Berard, a French Foreign Ministry official, who told Theodore Achilles, the US Chargé in Paris, on 2 May that the Colonel and Kidder had "not merely failed to try to restrain Diem but had encouraged him to take armed action."[96]

Did Lansdale disobey Collins' explicit orders to do everything possible to avoid conflict in his absence? This is a key question since an affirmative answer would show that the CIA operative took over US policy. Lansdale's personal account of what happened in the 28 April noon meeting with Diem reveals that he did not restrain Diem, and his confirmation of US support for the Prime Minister at this crucial juncture may have encouraged Diem to move against the Binh Xuyen. Kidder, who was also accused of encouraging Diem to attack the Binh Xuyen, believes that Lansdale did exactly this, as does Lucien Conein, a senior member of Lansdale's CIA team (known as the Saigon Military Mission) who collaborated closely with the Colonel in operations against the sect.[97] Also, on 3 May, Collins remarked at a Country Team meeting in Saigon that "somebody had fomented a revolution among the Americans,[98] and pointedly accused Lansdale of "inciting a mutiny."[99] This seemed to be confirmed by Homer Bigart in the *New York Times* on 22 August 1963 when he reported that Lansdale had sided with Diem against Collins, while Allen Dulles persuaded his brother (John Foster Dulles) that Lansdale had acted correctly.[100] However, evidence that could conclusively answer the above question remains in documents still classified by the CIA.

While Lansdale's messages caused the State Department to suspend action on replacing Diem, they did not result in the reversal of this policy. Though he had learned that the VNA had performed effectively, Dulles still did not know whether Diem would lose or would emerge as a hero, and, in fact, did not think the fighting "should hold up our planning." Allen Dulles agreed and, in a telephone conversation with the Secretary at 8:30AM on 28 April, state that the violence "takes us off the hook. It is better to make a change in the light of a civil war situation."[101]

While the US was prepared to await the result of the fighting Bao Dai was not. Concerned that the situation in Saigon might take a turn that would endanger his position, the Emperor ordered Diem and VNA Chief of Staff Ty, on 28 April, to report to Cannes for consultations to resolve the crisis, and delegated military powers to General Vy,[102] naming him Supreme Commander of the VNAF with authority to take all measures to avoid armed conflict between the VNA, the police and the sects.[103] Bao Dai also informed the US Embassy in Paris on 29 April that he was sending General Hinh to Saigon as his "special emissary." Hinh was to integrate sect forces into the VNA and the sects would obey Hinh once Diem was removed from the scene.[104] After receiving Bao Dai's telegram, Diem called Lansdale to the Palace on the afternoon of 29 April. The Colonel told the Prime Minister that "his real time of decision had come;" as a national leader had to think of the "larger good." At that moment, Nhu brought news that the Binh Xuyen radio was broadcasting the content of Bao Dai's telegram, which the Emperor had presumably made available to the sect. According to Lansdale, this was "the decisive straw" which made Diem choose to continue running the government and stay in Saigon.[105] On the same day Diem informed Kidder about his decision and issued a public statement declining to comply with Bao Dai's instructions.[106] Diem also refused to let Hinh enter the country and the General's plane had to land in Pnomh Penh.[107] VNA forces in Saigon under Colonels Minh and Tran Van Do backed Diem[108] and Vy fled to Dalat on 1 May.[109] Kidder did not object to Diem's stand but warned the Prime Minister that in disobeying Bao Dai's orders he was "undertaking an extremely grave responsibility." The French would certainly blame Diem for subsequent developments.[110]

The French did blame Diem for the outbreak of violence, but this time they also blamed the US. Ely told Kidder on 28 April that the fighting could have been avoided if the US had agreed to "some political solution" two or three weeks earlier. Ely condemned Diem for the crisis and accused the Prime Minister of insulting him many times[111] and spreading anti-French propaganda.[112] Diem was no longer head of a government, his position was illegal and Ely refused to remain in Vietnam if Diem continued as Prime Minister.[113] Aware that Collins was urging Diem's replacement in Washington and believing this to be US policy, Ely asked Kidder on 30 April whether the US would support the French in removing the Prime Minister. Kidder had just received the blocking cable from Dulles and did not know what US policy was, only that it was being formulated and that further instructions would follow. As Kidder described it: "I was left with no choice but to make up my own mind what our policy was and I would be damned if I was going to say I didn't know. With my legs shaking in my trousers... I told Ely 'No.'" Ely was "flabbergasted" and asked "How do you know that?" to which Kidder replied, "General, I know American foreign policy." Ely was "nearly hysterical."[114] Kidder also refused to join Ely in imposing a cease-fire on Diem as Collins had done at the end of March,[115] and his inaction allowed the Prime Minister to crush the Binh Xuyen and remain in power until US support was restored.

Thus, with *de facto* American backing and forces led by Colonel Minh and Thé, Diem was able to drive out the Binh Xuyen and gain control of Saigon-Cholon by 30 April. The fighting continued until 3 May, resulting in heavy casualties and widespread destruction. Five hundred persons were killed, two thousand wounded and twenty thousand lost their homes. Entire neighborhoods were flattened by artillery and mortar fire.[116]

With Diem's triumph assured and Congressional pressure to back him building up, Dulles, after wavering for three days, restored US support to the Prime Minister. When news of the fighting and Diem's success reached Washington, whatever influence Collins had with the Congressional Committees he had briefed, evaporated.[117] On 29 April Senator Mansfield made clear in a speech to the Senate that if Diem's government fell, the US "should consider an immediate supension of all aid to Vietnam and the French Union forces there..."[118] Senators William Knowland and Hubert Humphrey also backed Diem and, after listening to Collins, a large number of House Foreign Affairs Committee members informed the State Department through Congresswoman Edna Kelly that they did not want US support withdrawn from Diem.[119] On 1 May Dulles instructed Collins to indicate that the US was "supporting the Diem government to maintain its authority and to restore law and order." Collins was to restrain both Diem and the French from acting against each other and allow "indigenous and nationalist political forces... to work out a solution." Recent events, Dulles explained, had made Diem "a popular hero" and "a symbol of Vietnamese nationalism struggling against French colonialism and corrupt backward elements," while Bao Dai seemed to be siding with those forces. In light of Diem's success, US public and Congressional opinion was now "even less likely than before" to tolerate a forced removal of the Prime Minister. For the US to take part in such a scheme at this time would "be domestically impractical" as well as "highly detrimental to our prestige in Asia."[120]

Collins left the US on 29 April with instructions to remove Diem and landed in Saigon on 2 May to find US support restored to the Prime Minister. Faced with a *fait accompli*, the Ambassador had no choice but to adapt himself to the new situation until 14 May when he departed for Washington to be replaced by G. Frederick Reinhardt. In his final analysis, submitted on 5 May, Collins stated that Diem's victory over the Binh Xuyen would not "change his own basic incapacity to manage the affairs of government." In fact Diem's success would make it more difficult for the US to persuade him "to take competent men into [his] government... decentralize authority to his Ministers" and implement reforms properly. If this became clear, Collins advised that the US should either withdraw from Vietnam or find an "effective" Premier. Collins also stressed that no matter who headed the government, Vietnam could not be saved without the prompt and effective implementation of "sound political, economic and military programs" which required 'wholehearted agreement and coordination" between the Americans, French and Vietnamese. In the absence of such a "tripartite approach" Collins recommended that the US "should withdraw from Vietnam."[121]

Diem's victory, however, had made Dulles lose all interest in a "tripartite approach" and in cautious support for Diem. The Administration was convinced that Diem was the man to rule South Vietnam, and from now on US support for him would be complete and absolute without any conditions or reservations. As a result, Dulles decided that the time had come to take over completely from the French. He informed French Prime Minister Edgar Faure on 7 and 11 May in Paris that as a "nationalist anti-Communist force,"[122] Diem represented the "only means" to save South Vietnam,[123] and had to be given unconditional support.[124] Though Faure considered Diem "not only incapable but mad,"[125] he agreed to support the Prime Minister provided that the latter's government was broadened into "a real government of national union."[126] Dulles, however, rejected this condition, explaining that "in that part of the world there was no such thing as a coalition government but one-man governments."[127] The US could not give such guarantees "without turning Diem into a puppet and [a] total failure."[128] Dulles proposed instead that the two governments follow separate policies while informing each other of their general direction.[129] Faure agreed to disagree and thus ended both five years of Franco-American cooperation in Vietnam and the joint attempt to create a South Vietnamese state. Dulles wrote to Collins on 12 May that "the French government have now acquiesced in our point of view..." and instructed the State Department the next day to continue giving "complete, loyal and sincere support" to the "independent and sovereign" government of Diem.[130]

Diem's victory over the Binh Xuyen was the key event which secured his position for the next eight years by removing his main domestic opponents and convincing US policymakers of his indispensability. The fragmentation of US policy reflected in the Dulles/Lansdale-Collins split over Diem allowed him to act against the Binh Xuyen and thus proved crucial to his consolidation of power. Diem could not have survived without Lansdale's help, but the Colonel could not have saved Diem without Dulles. The Secretary's strong resistance to Diem's replacement delayed the Prime Minister's dismissal and brought Collins to Washington. Collins' departure suggested to Diem that the US was about to abandon him, while it also removed the main obstacle to Diem's move against the Binh Xuyen. By the time Dulles had accepted

Collins' advice, the Secretary's man in Saigon, Lansdale, had rendered the change in policy irrelevant.   Whether or not Lansdale actually encouraged Diem to act against the Binh Xuyen is less important than the fact that the CIA provided Diem with the means to achieve victory over the gangsters by splitting the sects so that the Binh Xuyen fought alone and by ensuring for Diem the critical military support of Colonel Duong Van Minh and Thé. Once Collins left, the time had clearly arrived for Diem to deal with the Binh Xuyen. Hence Dulles' prolonged refusal to act against Diem made it possible for Collins' detractors to save the Prime Minister in Saigon. All this showed the extent of US control over South Vietnam as well as the lack of coordination in US policy. It meant that the US attempted to replace and retain Diem at the same time. Thus, in hailing Diem's victory, the US was really applauding its own ability to outflank itself.

For a short time, the Administration did agree to replace Diem. Dulles accepted Collins' argument that US interest primarily required an effective government in Vietnam, which Diem could not create.   The Secretary agreed that there were nationalist alternatives to Diem and proved willing to override Mansfield's opposition when required. The restoration of US support for Diem on the other hand, betrayed the fact that US policy towards Vietnam was not based on a clear strategy but was formulated in reaction to particular events. The Administration retained Diem in power because his victory made it difficult to remove him. This by itself was understandable but Dulles overreacted to Diem's victory when he made renewed US support unconditional. Given that Diem's triumph did not invalidate Collins' main reason for wanting him replaced, this move seriously compromised the US' security interest.

This was the meaning of the triumph of Dulles' negative policy approach over Collins' positive one. Since November Collins had been arguing that Diem was setting up a dictatorship, not an effective government, and should therefore be replaced. Now Dulles made it clear that this did not matter as long as Diem was anti-French and anti-Communist; "one-man" governments, as Dulles told Faure, were the norm "in that part of the world." This statement, which "astounded" Faure,[131] revealed that the US was no longer interested in setting up an effective government in Vietnam. The contradiction in the aims of US policy which the Collins-Dulles debate over Diem had highlighted in December 1954, was now resolved in favor of the negative objectives. Unconditional support for a Diem dictatorship meant that the attempt to create a viable nation-state in South Vietnam was, in effect, abandoned by the US at the outset; from May 1955 on, American policymakers elected instead to put US prestige at the mercy of one man and a "non-nation,"[132] the demise of which even US forces could not ultimately prevent.

1   John L.S. Girling, *America and the Third World* (London: Routledge & Kegan Paul) 1980: 170.
2   Department of Defense, *US-Vietnam Relations 1945-1967*, Book 10 (Washington, DC) 1970: 731-741.
3   Department of State, Publication 6305, *South East Asia Treaty Organization.*
4   George M. Kahin, *Intervention: How America Became Involved in Vietnam* (New York: Knopf) 1986: 66.
5   *Foreign Relations of the United States*, (hereafter *FRUS*) 1952-1954, Vol. 13, Pt. 2 (Washington, DC) 1982: 1953, 1869.
6   *Ibid.*: 1957-1959.
7   *The Pentagon Papers*, Senator Gravel edition, Vol. 1 (Boston) 1971: 302.
8   Ronald H. Spector, *Advice and Support: The Early Years of the US Army in Vietnam, 1941-1960* (New York: Free Press) 1985: 225.
9   *The Pentagon Papers:* 219.
10   *FRUS*, 1952-1954, Vol. 13, Pt. 2: 2030.
11   *Ibid.*: 1980.
12   *Ibid.*: 1905-1909.
13   *Ibid.*: 2007-2009.
14   *Ibid.*: 1938-1939.
15   *Ibid.*: 2099.
16   *Ibid.*: 1955-1956.
17   *Ibid.*: 2130.
18   *Ibid.*: 2206, 2195.
19   David L. Anderson, "J. Lawton Collins, John Foster Dulles and the Eisenhower Administration's 'Point of No Return' in Vietnam," *Diplomatic History* 12:2 (Spring 1988): 130.
20   *FRUS*, 1952-1954, Vol. 13, Pt. 2: 2206.
21   *Ibid.*: 2239-2240.
22   *Ibid.*: 2368.
23   William C. Gibbons, *The US Government and the Vietnam War, Part I 1945-1960* (Princeton: Princeton University Press) 1986: 289.
24   *FRUS*, 1952-1954, Vol. 13, Pt. 2: 2272.
25   J. Lawton Collins, *Lightning Joe: An Autobiography* (Baton Rouge: Louisiana State University Press) 1979: 393.
26   *Ibid.*: 388.
27   *FRUS*, 1952-1954, Vol 13, Pt 2: 2363; J. Lawton Collins, interview by Richard D. Challener, 13 Jan 1966: 9, *Dulles Oral History Collection* (Princeton University Library).
28   *FRUS*, 1952-1954, Vol. 13, Pt. 2: 2379-2382.
29   *Ibid.*: 2419.
30   *FRUS*, 1955-1957, Vol 1 (Washington, DC) 1985: 3.
31   *FRUS*, 1952-1954, Vol 13, Pt. 2: 2401.
32   *Ibid.*: 2392.
33   *FRUS*, 1955-1957, Vol 1: 33.
34   *Ibid.*: 54-57.
35   *FRUS*, 1952-1957, Vol. 13, Pt. 2: 2401..
36   *FRUS*, 1955-1957, Vol. 1: 14.
37   *The Pentagon Papers:* 230.
38   George M. Kahin & John L. Lewis, *The United States in Vietnam* (New York: Delta) 1967: 70.

39 William S. Turley, *The Second Indochina War* (Boulder, CO: Westview Press) 1986: 14.
40 Bernard Fall, *The Two Vietnams: A Political and Military Analysis* (New York: Praeger) 1967: 245-246.
41 *FRUS*, 1955-1957, Vol. 1: 140.
42 *General Records of the Department of State*, Record Group No. 59, USAIRA to Washington, 30 March 1955, Lot Files, Box 1, File: Collins Mission Telegrams, December 1954-April 1955, National Archives, Washington, DC.
43 Edward G. Lansdale, *In the Midst of Wars: An American's Mission to Southeast Asia* (New York: Harper & Row) 1972: 267.
44 *FRUS*, 1955-1957, Vol. 1: 164-166.
45 *The Pentagon Papers:* 231.
46 *J. Lawton Collins Papers* (Vietnam File) [hereafter JLC Papers], Collins to Dulles, 30 March 1955, Telegrams sent March 25-31 1955, Box 31, Dwight D. Eisenhower Library (DDEL), Abilene, KS.
47 Collins: 401.
48 *FRUS*, 1955-1957, Vol. 1: 169.
49 Anderson, *Diplomatic History:* 133.
50 *FRUS*, 2955-1957, Vol. 1: 169-170.
51 *Ibid.:* 175.
52 *Ibid.:* 196.
53 *Ibid.:* 198.
54 *Ibid.:* 179.
55 *Ibid.:* 198.
56 *Ibid.:* 230.
57 *Ibid.:* 229.
58 *Ibid.:* 196.
59 *Ibid.:* 179.
60 *Ibid.:* 230.
61 *Ibid.:* 232.
62 *Ibid.:* 242-243.
63 *Ibid.:* 250-251.
64 *Ibid.:* 268-270.
65 Memorandum for the Record: South Vietnam—General Collins' Comments, 22 April 1955, *Office of the Special Assistant for National Security Affairs—Chronological Series*, Box 1, File April '55(6), DDEL.
66 *FRUS*, 1955-1957, Vol. 1: 280-287.
67 Collins: 405.
68 *FRUS*, 1955-1957, Vol 1: 294-298.
69 *Ibid.:* 301.
70 *Ibid.:* 306.
71 Joseph Buttinger, *Vietnam: A Dragon Embattled, Vol II: Vietnam at War* (New York: Praeger) 1967: 875-876.
72 Lansdale: 267-268.
73 Buttinger: 876.
74 *JLC Papers*, Telegram 4643, received from Paris, 25 Apr 1955, File: Monthly Papers April 1955 (3), Box 26, DDEL.
75 *JLC Papers*, Department of the Army, Staff Communications, Office Message, 24 Apr 1955, File: Telegrams received April 18-30, Box 32.
76 Kahin: 83.

77 Alfred W. McCoy, *The Politics of Heroin in Southeast Asia* (New York: Harper & Row) 1972: 124.

78 J. Davidson, *Indochina: Signposts in the Storm* (Kuala Lumpur: Logman) 1979: 99.

79 Lansdale: 274.

80 *FRUS*, 1955-1957, Vol 1: 291.

81 *State Records*, Telegram from Saigon to Secretary of State, 4827, April 27 1955, File 751G/4-2755.

82 Anderson, *Diplomatic History:* 39.

83 *FRUS*, 1955-1957, Vol 1: 303.

84 Anderson: 39.

85 *FRUS*, 1955-1957, Vol. 1: 300.

86 Lansdale: 283-284.

87 *Ibid.:* 277.

88 *FRUS*, 1955-1957, Vol. 1: 300.

89 Lansdale: 288.

90 Edward C. Keefer, *The US and the Consolidation of the Diem Government* (Unpublished Paper), Office of the Historian, US Department of State: 9.

91 *FRUS*, 1955-1957, Vol. 1: 305.

92 *Ibid.:* 302.

93 Lansdale: 289.

94 Keefer: 9-10; *FRUS*, 1955-1957, Vol. 1: 305-306.

95 *FRUS*, 1955-1957, Vol. 1: 305-306.

96 *Ibid.:* 352, fn.

97 Randolph Kidder, Letter to Author, 6 Oct 1988; Lucien Conein, Conversation with Author, 10 Sep 1989; Neil Sheehan, *A Bright Shining Lie: John Paul Vann and America in Vietnam* (New York) 1988: 139-140; Denis Warner, *Not With Guns Alone* (London) 1977: 105. Sheehan and Warner also state that Lansdale encouraged Diem to attack the Binh Xuyen.

98 Lansdale: 304.

99 Robert Shaplen, *The Lost Revolution: The US in Vietnam 1946-1966* (New York: Harper) 1966: 124; David Wise & Thomas B. Ross, *The Invisible Government* (New York: Random House) 1964: 157-158.

100 *New York Times*, 22 Aug 1963.

101 *FRUS*, 1955-1957, Vol. 1: 301, fn.

102 *JLC Papers*, Telegram 4928 from Saigon to State, April 29 1955, File: Monthly Papers April '55(5), Box 26.

103 *FRUS*, 1955-1957, Vol. 1: 316.

104 *Ibid.:* 335.

105 Lansdale: 299-300.

106 Buttinger: 833.

107 Collins: 406.

108 Spector: 249.

109 Buttinger: 833.

110 *FRUS*, 1955-1957, Vol. 1: 318.

111 *Ibid.:* 326.

112 *Ibid.:* 341.

113 *Ibid.:* 326.

114 Randolph Kidder, Unpublished Article (prepared for the State Department): 9-10.

115 *FRUS*, 1955-1957, Vol. 1: 316.

[116] McCoy: 119.
[117] Collins: 405.
[118]   *H. Alexander Smith Papers*, Mansfield Speech, 29 Apr 1955, Box 121, Princeton University Library.
[119] *FRUS*, 1955-1957, Vol. 1: 338.
[120] *Ibid.:* 344-345.
[121] *Ibid.:* 368.
[122] *Ibid.:* 397.
[123] *Ibid.:* 374.
[124] *Ibid.:* 405.
[125] *Ibid.:* 372-373.
[126] *FRUS*, 1955-1957, Vol. 1: 395.
[127] *Ibid.:* 399, fn.
[128] *Ibid.:* 401.
[129] *Ibid.:* 403.
[130] *Ibid.:* 405-6.
[131] Anderson: *Diplomatic History:* 143.
[132] Chester L. Cooper, *The Lost Crusade: America in Vietnam* (Greenwich, CT: Fawcett) 1972: 148.